5 MAR 2019

14

7

C153954376

Also by Douglas J. Findlay

WHITE KNEES BROWN KNEES

TAXI!

Never a Dull Day:
A Cabbie Remembers

DOUGLAS J. FINDLAY

BIRLINN

**KENT LIBRARIES
AND ARCHIVES**

C 153954376	
Askews	

First published in 2010 by
Birlinn Limited
West Newington House
10 Newington Road
Edinburgh
EH9 1QS

www.birlinn.co.uk

Copyright © Douglas J. Findlay 2010

The moral right of Douglas J. Findlay to be identified as the author of
this work has been asserted by him in accordance with the Copyright,
Designs and Patents Act 1988

All rights reserved. No part of this publication may be reproduced,
stored or transmitted in any form without the express written permission
of the publisher.

ISBN: 978 1 84158 896 4

British Library Cataloguing-in-Publication Data
A catalogue record for this book is available from the British Library

Typeset by Initial Typesetting Services, Edinburgh
Printed and bound by Bell & Bain Ltd., Glasgow

For a girl from Chippawa, Niagara Falls, Canada

JUST A THOUGHT

If you have driving skills and don't like people you can find a job as a lorry driver. On these seemingly eternal nocturnal hauls you need speak to no one. If however, you do like people, you can acquire a taxi. Who will you meet then? The rich, the famous and the desperate.

Quentin Crisp

CONTENTS

INTRODUCTION

Climbing the long flight of steps from Edinburgh's Waverley Station to Princes Street in November 1953, it dawned on me that I had better start thinking about my future. Finding a job should be my first priority. Less than sixty hours before I had been in my shorts, a member of the Middle East Air Force hating the heat and sun of Egypt, and now I was a civilian hating the freezing rain. Although a civilian, I was dressed in Air Force blue and laden with a kit-bag, a cardboard box containing my 'demob' suit. In addition the box contained a rubberised riding-coat, a trilby hat and a pair of brown shoes. Having worn black footwear for three years I felt in need of a change and had chosen a riding-coat because I thought it would provide protection when riding my trusty steed, a Speedwell bicycle. In lieu of the leave due to me that it had been impossible to take in Egypt, the RAF presented me with the princely sum of £28.10/–, so I felt rich.

Boarding the No. 6, the Marchmont Circle tramcar, I stowed my parcels under the stairs, and the conductor, no doubt in recognition of my deep tan, refused my proffered fare. Being ex-service himself he asked the inevitable question: 'When are you due back off leave?' It delighted me to be able to reply, 'Never.'

The soot-encrusted buildings confirmed that I was back in 'Auld Reekie' – Princes Street, Lothian Road and Tollcross were monochrome, only the green grass of the Meadows provided a splash of colour. We turned off Melville Drive into Marchmont

Road and I felt that nothing had changed during my time away. When we arrived at the first stop the conductor announced, 'Warrender Park Road – pianos and kippers!' At the next stop: 'Thirlestane Road – fur coats and nae drawers!'

We had a piano in our house and sometimes ate kippers, but of fur coats and the lack of nether garments I had no knowledge. I had been out of circulation for three years.

I decided that having a car would improve my chances of finding a well-paid job, so I looked through the *Evening News* and found there a 1928 Morris Minor for exactly £28.10/–. That I had no driving licence was not a problem as I was proficient on motor-cycles, and quite soon I passed my driving test and became street legal. My mother was a bit embarrassed, being chauffeured around in the old rattle-trap, and presented me with the money that I had allocated to her during my service.

I sold the old Morris for £28, suffering depreciation of only ten shillings, so it must have been fairly sound. My new car was a 1938 Standard Flying Nine, a two-door four-seater dream that ran like the proverbial sewing-machine.

I had a succession of poorly paid jobs and my financial position was precarious. It was then that I heard about a taxi company in Leith who were always on the lookout for drivers, so I made a beeline for their premises and was immediately taken on. The owner must have been as desperate for drivers as I was to drive. The fall of the flag* earned you two shillings, and, with luck and tips, it was possible to make a small profit. I was so keen on driving that I was content with a modest return for my labours. You could work the hours that suited you and most work came from inside the dock gates; as ships arrived with the tides, lots of night work was available.

Little did I know that driving a cab would broaden my experience of life to the extent that it did. I got into fights, met

---

* This refers to the action of switching on the taxi meter by pulling down the 'for hire' sign.

hooks, crooks and comic singers, found the inside of a police cell uninviting and even became friendly with a notorious madam who ran a brothel in central Edinburgh. I got to know and like a doctor with a sideline as an abortionist. I risked my life tangling with an ex-RAF policeman who murdered two people six weeks after our altercation. On the other hand, I rubbed shoulders with the salt of the earth and watched the world go by from the seat of my cab as I waited for fares.

In the pages that follow some characters appear in many tales, some others rate a single mention. In every case the stories are true, but the people involved are disguised, locations altered and chronological order is ignored.

For many years I entertained and possibly bored some with my taxi stories; but telling a tale, where you have the advantage of body language, and even bad language, is light-years away from writing amusing material. This book is my attempt at doing so. If it earns any money I will consider it to be delayed tips from my time as a long-suffering taxi driver. It doesn't matter whether it makes money or not; the only important thing is that you enjoy reading it.

Douglas J. Findlay
Glenesk, Canonbie Dumfriesshire

1

JOCK'S TAXI COMPANY

I forget who told me about Jock and his fledgling taxi company, but whoever he was, his information proved to be priceless as far as I was concerned. Driving was all I cared about, and if someone had asked me to drive around the world without pay I would have gladly accepted – so long as they stumped up for the petrol. Jock always needed drivers for his fleet of taxis, as he was the only operator providing a 24-hour service for the dockyards in Leith. His office was a ground-floor flat in a tenement within sight of the dock gates. Someone in the past must have agreed to let Jock park a taxi on the back green shared by the tenants and in time he had gradually taken over the whole area. Residents of the flats used to ask his permission to walk through his 'yard', and Jock, being a gentleman, would allow this privilege as long as it was infrequent. None of his taxis was less than twenty years old, with the majority well past their thirtieth birthday. About half of them were runners kept on the road by cannibalising the remainder. Some of the local courting couples would use Jock's older taxis, those without wheels but still wind- and weatherproof, to good effect. A more enterprising man might have rented them out, but Jock was not greedy.

Jock had little time for the authorities, and it was only after a serious warning from the police that he purchased one tax disc to cover his entire fleet; no one was sure about insurance. This state of affairs arose because inside the docks the law regarding motor vehicles did not apply. As long as one of Jock's taxis was used only to drive a passenger from his ship to the dock gates, he was fireproof. The obvious snag was how to get from his garage to the docks and back again and how to deal with a fare who wanted to ride from a ship to a bus depot or railway station up town. The answer was that you broke the law. Jock was a nice chap, although without doubt the biggest pirate operator in the city, and his activities were Nelson-eyed by the police and the rest of the taxi trade. When from time to time an ambitious sergeant or inspector would organise a crackdown, Jock's telephone would ring well in advance of the proposed raid and we would all be stood down for the duration. The one exception would be the cab with the tax disc.

When he offered me the chance to drive for him on a part-time basis he found in me a loyal and conscientious employee who served him well. In truth I was not an employee, since none of us were. We were self-employed, and Jock hired out his cabs to us at a shilling a mile. On leaving my day work at the tax office I would head for Jock's premises and drive for the fun of it, earnings being a secondary consideration. The old growler might be a museum piece fitted with solid spokes and an illegal meter, but it was transport. I was being gently introduced into a business that would not otherwise have entered my head. An added benefit was that after a night driving one of Jock's cabs my own car seemed to run like a Rolls Royce. In time I learned the ropes. If the hire was to a distant place the journey was via the taxi office, where the solitary tax disc would be handed over for that journey. If stopped by the police, the 'silly girl' in the office would be blamed for mixing up the discs. The system worked, and one morning at my day job, merely out of idle curiosity, I looked in vain for details of Jock's business being registered for taxation purposes. That was something else he had overlooked.

Jock's intelligence service on the shipping using Leith docks could have been sold to Lloyd's List. When a ship from any-where in the world tied up at any dock Jock's cabs would be waiting at any hour of day or night. A lot of the business was local traffic, and when a fishing trawler paid off, the taxi driver was guaranteed a decent tip and a nice piece of fish. I never quite knew what to do with the fish because it always had a head and a tail and bones and things like that.

I did hear a tale about fish and a TV star that made me smile. During the Festival a well-known performing artist, who later featured in the very successful TV series *That Was the Week That Was*, arrived in town. It turned out that his hobby was to hire a lady of the night from whom he demanded a peculiar service. When both were suitably disrobed she was obliged to pursue him round the room and thrash him with a wet fish. I had the lady concerned in the cab and she told me that he used her services a dozen times during the three weeks of the Festival. She was very enthusiastic about it and, as she explained, 'the fish was always fresh and when fried up afterwards it made a delicious supper.'

Another surprise was to discover that Leith had such a large number of girls of pretty easy virtue. I don't think that a fair person could have classified them as prostitutes, because their client base, if that is what it was, remained constant. When a ship arrived in port they would go on board and only disembark when it sailed again. When on board they were fed and accommodated and partied a lot on duty-free spirits and cigarettes. No doubt they would repair socks and wash and iron clothes as well. Whether they remained faithful to one ship or shipping line I didn't know, because there was so much coming and going that to me all the faces looked the same.

Jock knew weeks before anyone else that an American aircraft carrier was going to pay a goodwill visit to Edinburgh and would be parked overnight in Leith docks. We were desperate to keep it a secret and make our fortunes, but news like that inevitably leaked out. When the world's largest and second-best navy pays a visit to Scotland, it likes everybody to know about it. Goodwill tours to foreign parts keep the sailors happy. We were taken off driving for a night or two and it was all hands to the pumps in an endeavour to get as many as possible of Jock's taxis mobile. As the providers of regular transport to the docks, we hoped that some sort of favour would be shown to us, but it was not to be. Jock's fleet, a sorry-looking bunch at the best of times, held the head of the queue. It had been simple enough to gain the edge, as broken-down cabs were simply towed and pushed into position outside the dock gates a few days before the ship was due to arrive. Jock and his crew repaired and worked on them on the street, thereby securing the head of the queue for a dozen of Jock's more reliable vehicles.

On the great day Jock had us on parade at four o'clock in the morning in case the matelots were released early. We seemed to have the place to ourselves, and with mounting excitement we began to count our chickens. We had dollar signs before our eyes and the tax office even granted me a day's leave because my granny had died again, unexpectedly. The burning question was – where were the sailors? As the time passed, more and more taxis joined the queue. At this rate we would be lucky to get a single fare out of it. Finally, long after dawn had broken and elevenses had been served, the only taxis not lined up outside the docks were those of drivers who were on the sick list. Edinburgh was empty of cabs. The first liberty boat had been scheduled to land at six in the morning but had still not put in an appearance. Before then some of the wiser cabbies had called it a day and headed south into the city looking for guaranteed business. At a few minutes after eleven a local policeman, aided by some dock-yard police, put in an appearance. They herded us like sheep in a snake-like trail into the docks and back out again to the exit gates where we waited and fretted. We had waited so long that peace broke out between licensed and unlicensed operators. It was agreed that we would charge a levy of two pounds on top of the clock fare on each journey. In this way we would compensate for lost time. It would be quite legal to do this, since we would be inside the docks when we picked up our passengers and struck our bargains and therefore out of the jurisdiction of the police-controlled Cab Office.

At last, a sea of snow-white sailors' hats bobbed towards us. Glory Be! Some trade at last. Six jolly jacktars, determined to enjoy a shore leave together, tumbled into my cab. I started to explain that the limit was five passengers only, when at last my brain clicked into gear. We were inside the docks, so the rules did not apply and I surrendered quickly. Somewhere in US naval circles there was a high-ranking official who distrusted taxi drivers, and when this man gave orders they had to be obeyed. We crept to the exit gate where two huge American snowdrops swinging their Billy clubs in an ominous manner were joined by two dockyard police in support of them and to keep things UK legal. They inspected each cab as it passed through the gates. I knew that one of my passengers would be ejected. As I stopped at the gate the larger shore-patrol man opened one of the cab doors.

'OK, boys,' he drawled. 'Behave yourselves or you'll be in the Brig before you know what hit you.' I breathed a sigh of relief and prepared to drive off. Before I could drop the clutch he added, 'It's a dollar to the city centre – got that?' And he looked at a bobby to confirm the rate. One of Leith's finest nodded in agreement and my passengers paid close attention to the advice. Over seven hours' wait and we were to get a measly dollar to Princes Street! The entire exercise had been a waste of time. Four hundred yards from the dock gates we approached the bottom of Leith Walk.

'Stop the cab, buddy.' The order came from the back seat. 'Is that an English pub?' I kept my mouth shut but nodded in agreement because now was not the time to point out that they were in Scotland and not England. He and his buddies had seen the lights in the pubs twinkling and noticed girls nudging each other and pointing out the presence of strange white sailor suits in the passing taxis. They quite rightly assumed that publicans and girls would both welcome their arrival even if it was before noon. The only mistake they made was in presuming that the bottom of Leith Walk was Edinburgh's city centre.

'This will do us just fine. We want to meet some girls.' As they dismounted, each in turn handed me a single dollar bill. I was a bit miffed about no tip but I have always been a bit of an Oliver Twist. I was back in the queue awaiting more passengers within minutes, and my second consignment of only five this time was anxious to know where I had dropped their buddies. Five dollars later I was back in the queue again. By now the queue of available cabs had dwindled. Some unfortunate drivers arriving in Princes Street had been paid off with a single dollar, and they gave up and decided to concentrate on regular trade. Jock's supporters soldiered on. I had got the hang of it now and whenever my passengers asked me to advise them of a lively spot I dropped them off at the bottom of Leith Walk and held my hand out for a dollar from each passenger. All good and bad things come to an end and the liberty boats eventually stopped arriving.

Having nowhere else to go I decided to hang around. The bank manager would be delighted. My last passenger was a solitary sailor who seemed to me to be better educated than any of the others I had driven.

'Where to sailor?' I had adapted to the vernacular.

'Dublin please.' The reply was matter-of-fact.

'DUBLIN?'

'Yes. Dublin, you know, it's in Ireland.' I was dumbfounded.

'Do you know how far it is?' It was a reasonable request.

'Yeah, I looked it up on the way across. It's only that much away.' At that he held up finger and thumb to illustrate a distance of about half an inch.

'How long is your shore leave?' I looked questioningly at him.

'It's until midnight.' It was time to break the sad news and he was very disappointed. 'Gee,' he said. 'I got kin-folk over there called O'Malley. Have you heard of them?' He was adamant that we could get there and back before midnight. 'I know there's a ferry, so can we not get that?'

Eventually he accepted the position. If his leave had been a weekend we would have been off to Stranraer before he could say 'St Patrick'. He settled for a view of Dublin Street, a look at Edinburgh Castle, followed by a quick trip round Arthur's Seat and then a visit to a pub, where he sampled Guinness for the first time. I don't think he liked it. I also introduced him to a product new to the British market, Golden Wonder crisps, which he insisted on calling chips. When I explained chips he insisted that what I was talking about were fries.

Apart from speaking two different languages we got along famously. He was my best fare of the day and he still had time to spare and money to spend.

George Melly, who was to become internationally acclaimed as a jazz singer, was then a slip of a lad. He dressed entirely in black and carried a coffin on to the stage where he was wowing the audiences in the Usher Hall. The coffin gimmick linked to the Saint Louis Blues Funeral March played by Mick Mulligan's Magnolia Jazz Band always brought the house down. The staid Scots thought his outrageous behaviour the best thing since sliced Hovis. Having seen the show myself I knew that my new friend would have a good evening if he added a visit to the show to his itinerary. When he heard the names Melly and Mulligan, he immediately decided that they were Irish, and I did not dissuade him because I didn't really know myself where they were from. 'Hey,' he enthused, 'perhaps that Melly guy is kin-folk of mine. Gee, I'm sure glad I got your cab. I feel that I've been to the old country already. After the show I'll go back-stage to meet him because there's just a chance he'll know my cousins.' He was completely convinced that everyone would know everyone else in a tiny place like Ireland.

I was sorry to discover that few sailors seemed to take taxis back to the ship since I had to go back to Leith to hand in the old taxi to Jock. Our proprietor was in his element and his rate of exchange from dollars to pounds was very much in his favour. I trusted my bank a little more than I did Jock, so that was where my stash of dollars finished up. Jock's sharp dealings and his hard work surely paid off, because in later years he was the first cab operator in Leith to introduce two-way radios to his fleet of – by then – quite decent taxis.

In the early days, when I still had a lot to learn, the office sent me to the docks to pick up a fare to the Caledonian Station at the west end of Princes Street. Jock insisted that it was an ideal opportunity to take a turn 'up town' to see if any trade could be poached. This meant entering enemy territory, but needs must, as the saying goes. I could have dropped the fare off outside the station, but I wanted to study the opposition, so I drove inside. I was working hard to gain the necessary knowledge of the city's topography in order to sit my test for a proper taxi driver's licence by this time. When I passed the exam it would be easy enough to get a job, as even a part-time one would do, driving a black cab. It was the pinnacle of my ambition at that time, and the thought that one day I might become an owner-driver never crossed my mind.

Sailors home from the sea are generally excellent fares, and this one was no exception to the rule; the tip was more than the fare on the clock. I was flushed with success. Even the hostile and scornful glances from the cabbies, regular patrons of the station café who were milling about outside it, left me unaffected and I ignored them completely. They were keen to ensure that a pirate did not pick a fare up from a rank their association had purchased, and which rightly belonged to them, and I had no intention of even trying it on. I would inevitably meet them again and they would doubtless have long memories. Despite having been on active service, I am not really hero material. I toyed with the idea of parking up and chancing my arm by buying a cup of tea in their canteen, just to experience the reaction, but chickened out. Instead I parked outside the station and walked the 50 yards to the Rutland Hotel, a place that I had previously visited on the rare occasions when my pockets were full. The result would be a life-changing experience.

Standing next to me at the bar was a small, stocky individual whose name, he duly informed me, was Paul, and we chatted about this and that. He had no idea that I was a pirate driver and I had no idea that he was a licensed cab owner. Naturally it came out in the wash and we bought each other drinks and discussed the taxi trade. Paul eventually told me that he was a regular at the hotel and suggested that I look him up when I passed my street test, as he was on the lookout for a driver so that he could have more free time. He was a shrewd cookie and knew that a new dog would not know any of the old tricks. I would believe everything that he told me and his money and investment would be safe. I was not much of a drinker and after far too many lagers and lime I left to make my way back to Leith in the dark. Far too many for me at that time were perhaps three or four half pints, and well below the drink drive limit in those pre-breath-test days, but I did feel the effects of the alcohol.

When I climbed into the old taxi and prepared to drive off I was made aware that two ladies were sitting on the back seat.

'Glengyle Terrace, if you please, driver,' I was instructed in a rather imperious tone. I started to protest and was about to explain that a booking would have to be made through the office in Leith, but was cut short. 'Don't be ridiculous, driver. There are no taxis in the station and we have had to come out into the street to find you. Please carry on.' This was long before the new one-way system was put into operation and taxis turned right as they exited the station. My cab was facing towards Rutland Square, and I decided that the most direct route would be via Rutland Square, Canning Street, Morrison Street, Lothian Road and Home Street, and there it would be. A slightly longer journey, but it would avoid traffic and therefore be much quicker. It was sheer chance that the Tollcross area was the one I was currently studying and that I knew where to find the address. As I drove ahead past the station exit the two ladies in the back instantly decided that I was taking them the long way round to increase the fare, and pointed this out to me. I shouted above the din that

I was taking them by the shortest route as would be proved by the fare when we got there. They presumably glowered in reply but certainly said nothing that I could hear.

The best of Jock's old cabs was a bone-shaker, and this was one of his oldest. We rattled round the corners, and even in my fuddled state I noticed that the old car was swinging her back end about rather a lot. By the time we got to Morrison Street the volume of noise from the ladies was even louder than the roar of the engine and the rattles of the bodywork and I finally heard their chorus of protests.

'Let us out. Let us out this minute. This taxi is a death trap.' I thought this a bit unfair on someone who was breaking the law to help them, but they were right. A flat tyre was the problem, and the fact that I had not really noticed it gives an idea of how much of a rattler Jock's old cab was. They stormed off without the slightest offer of a fare, never mind a tip. Jock did not equip his fleet with spare wheels, in case of theft by his staff, and it was some considerable time before I managed to get back to his office in Leith. By then I was as sober as the proverbial judge.

Naturally I vowed never to touch alcohol again when I was anywhere near a cab, but the fickle finger of fate was to lay a trap for me, and sure enough, I was to blunder into it.

2

THE SRA

Someone described the weather conditions as an aberration, which was a safe description because nobody quite knew what it meant. A clinging wet low fog had enveloped the whole area of the city. I had completed an unsuccessful trip to Leith docks, where conditions were so awful that no ships were arriving or departing. A series of mournful foghorns let us know the direction in which the inward-bound ships lay at anchor, fearful of a collision. I knew the docks well but took my life in my hands while trying to turn Jock's old taxi round on one of the quays. I had no idea of exactly where I was. The brakes on Jock's old bangers were dangerously poor when driving forward and virtually non-existent when reversing. To turn round I was in and out of the cab several times to ensure that I was not liable to fall into the icy cold, black, oil-covered waters of the dock. Not a soul was about and it was clearly a night for huddling round the fire. This brought its own problems. Auld Reekie was well-named, since the soot from thousands of coal fires rose to merge with the down-draught of wet air, creating a dirty layer of atmosphere that coated anything and everything in its path. It was not like any rain that I had previously experienced, but was more like dirty clouds at zero feet. The windscreen wipers could not cope, and as quickly as they swept one way across the screen the clean area was instantly re-soaked with filthy muck, resulting in an almost completely restricted view.

Jock, from the warmth of his home-cum-office, had come up with a bright suggestion when he reported: 'I've just heard on the wireless that the Corporation has withdrawn all bus services due to the hazardous conditions, so you can go up town and try your luck. Half the cabs will be off the road as well, so you will be able to make a small fortune.' I was not so sure. The conditions were dire and some public houses had closed their doors early as they were getting no custom worth speaking about. But I was young and eager so I decided to give it a try.

The orange sodium street lamps appeared to have a halo round them as I drove slowly up Leith Walk. It was a strange experience, because, although I knew full well that there were shops or tenements and houses on each side of the street, I could see nothing of them, not even lighted windows. Very little of the overhead light reached street level, so that the taxi was in the dark for twenty or thirty yards, then we entered an area of gloom for a few yards, before plunging into darkness again. When I reached the Pilrig junction I was forced to stop because the traffic lights, complete with different-coloured haloes, were against me. It was an eerie feeling to be completely alone at what was usually a very busy junction.

I peered around in vain for potential passengers, and as the traffic lights switched to green I was just moving off when I thought I felt the old growler sink down on its nearside. A second later I distinctly heard the click of the door being closed. I glanced round to see who had boarded the cab but there was no one there. Now, I don't believe in ghosts, and if I did, then they would not require a door to gain access to a cab, and as spirits they would be weightless – but the taxi had definitely dipped to one side. Was my mind playing tricks? Surely not; I had definitely heard the door-lock click. I quickly made a double-check and would have turned on the inside light, but as usual with Jock's taxis the bulb had disappeared, no doubt cannibalised to meet an urgent need elsewhere. There was no one there that I could see, so something funny was going on and I was about to pull over to make a proper inspection when a voice from the rear instructed, 'Don't pull the flag, just keep on going, your fare will be settled.'

Now that I knew I was dealing with a human being and not an unseen force I became much more confident and glanced into the back to identify my passenger, but there was still no one to be seen. The voice of my invisible passenger in the back continued: 'Are we being followed? Can you see any cars behind us?' The answers, after a quick check, were 'no', and a second 'no'. In the short time that I had been driving a taxi I had been waiting to be told to 'follow that cab', and this ran it close. I checked again in my misted-up mirrors and peered about, but the streets were clear and I seemed to be the only car in town. I addressed the invisible man.

'I can't see any cars and the buses are all off the road, so what am I looking for?'

'Double-check again.' The command was urgent. 'A motorcycle or perhaps even a pedal cyclist. Can you be absolutely sure that we are not being followed?' I assured him that we were completely alone. 'Take a left,' he demanded, and as I dutifully turned into Brunswick Street I pulled the flag on the meter down and reminded him that he owed me for some unregistered distance. He was reassuringly dramatic. 'Don't worry about money; you'll earn good wages before this night is out.' By now my fare had risen from his hiding place on the floor, close against the partition between the front and the back cabin and was sitting on the back seat. His head swivelled from side to side to check for himself that the streets were indeed clear. He then introduced himself.

'I'm the Regional Commander of the Scottish Republican Army Southern Command and I've been instructed to inspect the border defences. We've a long night ahead of us.'

'The Borders?' My voice had risen by at least an octave. 'Do you mean Peebles and Galashiels or the real border at Carlisle and Newcastle?'

'Yeah,' he responded. 'That sort of place, but I can't tell you too much because it is top secret classified information.' I awaited his confirmation of our destination but he failed to reply. 'I'd better start for Fairmilehead then?' Again he failed to answer. He had not spotted my deliberate mistake in suggesting Newcastle instead of Berwick-on-Tweed as being the Scottish border. To my mind he had no idea of where he wanted to go. Instead of answering me, or even listening to me, he sat with his head moving from side to side, peering out of the back window into the blackness of the night. He was intent on discovering a car following us, but we had the road to ourselves.

'It's the police,' he whinged. 'Special branch have me under constant surveillance so I have to be alert at all times.' That night, I could only surmise, Special Branch had been negligent and slipped out to the pub or home like sensible plods. If they were not a figment of his imagination it was clear that he had given them the slip. My worries were slowly increasing that I just might have a lunatic on board, and, besides, Jock's old taxi was getting homesick for the sounds of the sea. It could have been years since it had last had a run in the countryside, and I had visions of breaking down miles from anywhere. I reverted to the taxi driver's old standby.

'If we're going to be out all night I'll need to fill up with petrol, and I've only just come on duty, so I'll have to ask you to pay me some of the fare up front.' A distinct change came over the Regional Commander of the Scottish Republican Army.

'Ah well, it's like this. The treasurer owes me quite a bit of money that I've spent on guns and training volunteers and that, and I've not got much on me. We'll have to go back home to pick up some cash. But before we do that, go to the start of the Biggar road and I'll signal that we've been delayed.'

The climb up the road at that point is hardly noticeable in a modern car, but Jock's old taxi had an asthma attack as it tried to drag itself up the slope. After a couple of hundred yards of the old growler growling away in protest at the unfamiliar exertion, it was on the point of giving up the ghost when I was instructed to stop. My passenger alighted and pointed a torch towards Loanhead. This he assured me was towards the eyes of the 'south', where unseen watchers would be awaiting his signal. He flashed his torch four times but no answering signal was received. I suggested that we approach some of the unseen watchers with a request for some cash, as this would save not only time but the risk of being spotted by Special Branch if we visited his home. He solemnly advised me that it was as much as my life was worth for me to meet any of the members of a second cell. I had a thought that the Regional Commander's rightful place was in a padded one, but kept my views to myself, although it later transpired that my view was not exclusive. He returned to the back seat highly pleased with himself and we trundled back to Leith.

He lived in the ground floor flat of a tenement in Dickens Street, and as he left the cab to collect some money I invited myself indoors with him. There was no way that he was going to do a runner across the back greens. It seemed strange to me that he did not have a key to his own front door but was obliged to ring the doorbell to gain admittance. In a few moments a lady answered the door. She had a worried look on her face and catching sight of us her eyes shot heavenwards. 'Oh no,' she groaned aloud, 'not again.' Looking at me standing behind him she added, 'Don't tell me you've been riding about in taxis again.' After a short pause she observed. 'You'd better come in because we can't let the neighbours hear this nonsense.'

The Regional Commander was in a buoyant mood.

'Come on, hen,' he coaxed, 'give the guy ten or fifteen pounds. He's sound, fully trustworthy. Come on.' He might as well have talked to the wall for all the notice she paid him. She was very presentable, clearly well educated and obviously sick to death of her husband's crazy antics. She addressed herself directly to me.

'He's quite mad you know. Certifiable. His head is full of this SRA rubbish. Why don't you drop him off at Craiglockhart where he belongs?' With that outburst over she sat down on the settee, opened her *Scotsman* newspaper and pretended to read it in a rather ostentatious manner. It was as if the whole thing had nothing to do with her, which I suppose it hadn't. The SRA Chief had other ideas. He leaned over his wife's reading material and wheedled away.

'Come on, darling, just a few measly quid. When we take over I'll be an MP at least, if not a minister. Come on and help me out.' As he was speaking he slipped a cigarette lighter out of his pocket, lit it, and held the naked flame against her newspaper, which obligingly caught fire. I admired his wife tremendously. She held the flaming newspaper as long as possible and I can assure you that the sight was quite alarming; eventually, when the flames reached ceiling-height, she dropped the burning debris onto the carpet, where I gallantly stamped it out.

She turned to me and rather unnecessarily pointed out, 'There you are, what did I tell you? He's as mad as a hatter.' She was not the least bit excited or alarmed and her voice was calm and reasoned; she clearly knew what she was talking about. 'I suppose that I should be thankful that he's not violent. But that said, he is quite, quite mad.' Eventually she took pity on me. 'I know that it's not your fault. Wait a minute.' With that she located her handbag, fumbled in it and presented me with two one-pound notes. 'Will that cover the damage?' It would have to do, so it did. I had wasted a lot of time but not run all that many miles. On a cost-per-mile basis it was the best night's work that I had done for Jock for ages. I thanked her profusely and gave a curt nod of goodbye to the Regional Commander.

By the time I had settled up with Jock I was still in pocket but I had to admit that it had been a bit scary. Then again, I was learning all the time, and I certainly had a lot to learn about this strange business. Before I departed for some well-earned rest I decided to consult Jock and tell him the tale of the SRA and one of its senior members.

'What!' cried Jock in disgust, 'You mean to tell me that you had the Regional Commander of the Scottish Republican Army in one of my cabs and you let him off with a measly two pounds? You must be as crazy as he is. Why, on a good night, when he's got hold of some money he's good for twenty quid minimum.'

When taxi-driving you meet many idiots, but finding a wealthy one is a rare experience. When discovered they should be husbanded, cared for and above all, exploited.

3

CHARLIE THE GANGSTER

Although Charlie was to play an almost welcome role in my life at a much later date, I know that he travelled on very few occasions in my cab. Charlie was much more of a Charlie than a gangster, and since his surname rhymed with gangster the moniker is easily explained. He was neither big nor tough, but imagined that he was until he discovered his error. His main claim to fame was that he looked so ordinary that his victims had great difficulty in trying to identify him when shown photographs of possible suspects in police identity records. Almost invariably they shook their heads and failed to recognise him. According to Charlie people were afraid to recognise him, but the fact remains that he was very ordinary-looking.

He was determined to carve out a career for himself as a criminal and had decided that pocket-picking and pimping off his wife would be his chosen route. He was also prepared to take part in other gangsterish pastimes just so long as the risk was limited. Very early on he discovered that his skill as a 'dip' was minimal, so he concentrated his efforts on robbing his wife's clients. Although she was quite an attractive girl, the customers that she took back to their home were invariably drunk. While the punter was enjoying the delights afforded by his wife, Charlie would rifle the pockets of the client's discarded trousers. As often as not the robbery took place while the unfortunate man was sleeping off his excesses. Charlie considered this an extremely successful way to conduct business. It was virtually risk-free for him. While he was away with the money, Mrs Charlie had to face the outrage of the former house guest when he sobered up, and it was she who received the black eyes on behalf of her ever-loving.

He used my taxi only a couple of times, and each time I was a bit uncomfortable having him aboard because he was a person who attracted trouble and it could flare up at any time. To refer to yourself as 'Charlie the Gangster' is not very sensible unless you enjoy confrontation, and all the two-bit budding hard cases were queuing up to have a pop at him. They did this in the hope of making a name for themselves, but his scalp was value-less. Charlie lacked the courage to be a proper thief and lost all credibility when his pint of beer was poured over his head in a bar one evening and he failed to retaliate. It transpired that he owed the man money, and when repayment was demanded he reneged. Charlie's version of events was quite different from the rumours circulating about him. As far as he was concerned, he was a man of honour. It was, he acknowledged, a pity that he had a cash flow problem at that particular moment. Why, he had even offered a practical solution in proffering the ser-vices of his wife in exchange for the trifling sum due. That the creditor had refused such generous terms was proof positive that he was mad, and it was unwise to fight with a lunatic, since it is common knowledge they have the strength of ten men. As far as the beer incident was concerned, it was not quite a full pint as he had already drunk some of it. The success of his pocket-picking and his wife's business enterprise can be gauged by the fact that they both drew unemployment benefit from the state. I was to meet Charlie and his wife again in most curious circumstances.

It was just after one in the afternoon when I was called to a ship-ping office in Leith, where my fare was a very smartly dressed young man aged about twenty who walked with a pronounced limp. He gave me very strange and precise instructions.

'Take me to where I can find a woman will you, driver, please.' This solicitation was more to be expected late at night from the odd drunk than from the sober young type sitting in the back of the taxi.

'Sorry, sir,' was my stock reply. 'I don't carry the stick but I can drop you at the Deep Sea and you can take a chance there. It's very early, so there will be few women about and it is a bit risky.'

A word of explanation may be required. To 'carry the stick' was taxi-driver parlance for those who help others to find loose women. The allusion is to assisting the blind by carrying their white cane for them. To be caught or even to be accused of doing so could lose a driver his good name or, worse yet, his taxi plate. Although certain operatives did 'carry the stick', it was done very discreetly. The young bloke in the back was full of the joys of spring and anxious to hit the town, and his pockets were obviously full. He was certainly no policeman, since he was far too young and his feet were of normal size.

'That'll be fine, mate. Anywhere that I can find a bit of stuff.' Without prompting he went on to explain. 'I've just been flown home from South America by my shipping line and I'm going to have a smashing leave.' It was news to me that ships' crews were being flown round the world, but I had no reason to doubt his word. As we drove up Leith Walk he informed me that he had suffered an accident when he'd fallen down into the hold of his ship. After being patched up in a local hospital it was clear that he would need a few weeks or months of rest and recovery time, and he had been sent home. His pockets were bulging with back pay, sick-leave money and an advance of compensation, and he was eager to spend it. 'If I don't get into bed with a bird this afternoon I'm that famous Dutchman Rick Van Edam,' he boasted. As I was fairly sure that I was a few years his senior I took it on myself to counsel caution.

'Listen, Jack.' All seamen were referred to as Jack and he was quick to introduce himself as Bob. 'If I were in your shoes I would pace myself. Have a couple of drinks and then wait until tonight. All the dance halls will be open and you will be able to find a nice girl to spend your leave with.' He failed to find my suggestion attractive.

'Not on your Nellie.' He was bubbling over with excitement. 'I'll tell you what I'll do. Since I can't walk too well I'll hire you as my driver for a couple of days. How about it?' A deal was done but I still could not help him in his quest. 'If you pick me up here on the corner of Picardy Place at four o'clock we can see what's on the cards. Maybe have a meal or something.' He paid me five pounds up front, which was very trusting of him, and I left him to his adventures. Five pounds was a lot of money, but despite the windfall I went off to earn another shilling or two.

At four o'clock I was waiting for him and he turned up promptly with a fairly attractive youngish woman in tow.

'I told you I'd get to bed this afternoon,' were his first words. It was more of a declaration than a confidential whisper. The girl blushed modestly as Bob went on. 'I didn't get to bed really; it was only a knee trembler, but we're going to bed now.' The address that I was to go to was a hovel at the very bottom of the Royal Mile. It was unusual inasmuch as it was at the top of a short flight of open steps. The house still showed signs of damage caused by an explosion of some sort. It was claimed that it was the one that killed Lord Darnley in Scotland's own gunpowder plot, but I was pretty sure from my history lessons at school that the site of the blast that killed the unfortunate Lord was at Kirk o' Field, which was located somewhere between Infirmary Street and Chambers Street. In any event, Darnley was buried in 1567, and if he was connected with the house at the foot of the Canongate it proves how slow the council's maintenance programme must be in that area of the town. I picked them up again at seven and they visited a few public houses before returning to the love nest.

He was a considerate employer, and between drop-off and pick-up I was free to work and I was entrusted with his roll of notes each night. Sometimes his permanent flame would introduce a second girl to spice up his love life and his roll of notes slimmed down daily. Bob had become a bit of a fixture at the 'Canongate cottage', as he called it, and it came to light that his paramour was none other than Mrs Charlie the Gangster. Charlie would join them late at night when his gangstering was done for the day and the three of them would sleep happily together. Bob complained that it was a bit of a tight squeeze when one of the extra girls stayed over, but he was prepared to put up with it. In the mornings they breakfasted together and it must have been a very homely arrangement. Charlie was foiled in any attempt to rob Bob because I was his overnight banker. My taxi was kept busy running from bar to brothel and back again. All good things come to an end, especially when the money runs out, and when Bob's did he went out of my life as quietly as he had come into it.

Before we shook hands for the last time I thought it my duty to give him a few more fatherly words of advice.

'Now, Bob,' I counselled, 'you've had your fun, but you must have run some terrible risks. If I were you I'd go to the Royal Infirmary for a check-up at the Social Diseases Clinic; it's off the Middle Meadow Walk. Better to be safe than sorry.' Bob looked at me as if I were a simpleton. He was mentally a lot older than his claimed nineteen years. Without a word he rolled up his trouser leg to show that he was still bandaged from ankle to thigh.

'When I fell on that rusty old iron it tore my leg all the way up. They had to fill me with penicillin to prevent blood poisoning – millions of units every day for weeks on end. The MO said that I couldn't catch a dose of the pox if I tried.'

Bob was a cool customer and I surmised that he had stolen a few days from his sick leave to enjoy his high jinks. He would no doubt now be bound for hearth and home, where his family would cosset him and be regaled with tales of far-off places. I doubted he would mention his adventures much nearer home in Edinburgh at the Canongate cottage!

I never saw or heard of Bob again, but Charlie the Gangster would, like a bad penny, turn up again.

4

BERNARD

Bernard was a third-generation scrap merchant descended from Irish gypsy stock, and he lived in a caravan sited inside the gates of his main premises with his devoted wife and a small tribe of little Bernard and Bernadette lookalikes. From six in the morning till midnight he dispensed fuel from the petrol pumps outside his yard. When he slept and sired his large family was anyone's guess. He owned several depots in the area and the post-war government disposal of War Department vehicles and spares had made him extremely rich. A stranger would never guess as much, judging by Bernard's appearance; flat cap, dungarees and wellingtons. Cars and vans were piled on top of each other in his various yards, and they must have numbered several hundred, yet at any hour, seven days a week, Bernard could advise not only where a car was located but also whether it still had the part a customer was seeking.

On the few occasions that Bernard was absent from his main yard in Leith his ever-pregnant wife stood in for him. Her knowledge of the stock was not quite as encyclopaedic as his, but she was a shrewd businesswoman. Neither husband nor wife was keen on paper work and it is possible that reading and writing skills had been set aside in the successful pursuit of wealth. Bernard was not much of a talker either, and his catch phrase, 'nae bother', seemed to cover most of his communication needs.

Someone in the organisation must have been employed to scan the press, because Bernard was always aware of where bargains would be found. His latest bulk purchase was a fleet of fifty trucks, complete with large round metal tanks still camouflaged in desert sand and brown paint. There was a steady demand for the 15-cwt ex-army trucks, but no one wanted them when fitted with the metal tanks that made up the deal, so Bernard picked them up as a job lot for a song. Only he was sharp enough to realise that they had been fresh-water bowsers in a former life and were constructed of top-quality heavy gauge copper. When they were taken off the trucks and melted down Bernard had made not a killing but a massacre. He could have given the trucks away for free, but the word 'free' was not in his vocabulary. When he related the tale of his good fortune he insisted that it had all been 'nae bother'.

Had it not been for his use of 'nae bother' I doubt whether I would have recognised the smartly suited gentleman who hailed my taxi. I was still driving for Jock at that time, and a fare from Leith to Fairmilehead and back was an unusual treat. We were headed for a salvage sale being run by a government agency. Bernard was going to be a late arrival, since the sale was scheduled to commence at noon, and it was now nearly three o'clock. When we got there we parked up, and as I was at a loss for something to do, I decided to accompany Bernard and watch his every move. He was a successful man and a free lesson is always good value. The sale was an alfresco affair and a discouragingly cold wind was blowing from the north. We hung around and chatted away until the last lot of the day was called. It was a vast collection of old hospital equipment: beds, chrome stands for this and that, some old X-ray equipment, trolleys minus the odd wheel, and a pyramid of metal-framed chairs and tables and a few ancient dentists' couches.

'Number 416 in the catalogue, gentlemen, a miscellaneous assortment of obsolescent hospital equipment. You could ship it to Africa and set up a clinic and make a fortune,' the auctioneer beamed at his witticism, which was lost on the crowd of possible bidders. 'Now, gentlemen, there's so much of this stuff that I'm not even going to try to separate it into lots. I'll sell it all in one go. Who'll open the bidding? Shall we say a thousand? A thousand pounds anywhere? A thousand pounds to start me off?' He might as well have talked to the trees. 'All right. Five hundred then? Five hundred pounds for all this stuff; there must be tons of it. Come along. It's the bargain of the sale and it has got to go.' A long silence followed this plea. 'All right. Have it your way. I'll start at two hundred and fifty pounds. Who'll give me a bid?' His tone was now wheedling. Finally he capitulated. 'Right then,' he began again brightly, 'one hundred pounds,' and he added the warning, 'I'm going to sell. Make no mistake.' He looked around expectantly as the sparse audience looked anywhere but at him. 'Make me an offer then.' By now he sounded really desperate. My companion spoke. Not many words, but they did constitute a bid.

'A pound, give me a pound and I'll take it away for you.' The man with the hammer was nonplussed.

'What do you mean, sir? You'll take it away for a pound? This is an auction. We don't pay you money. The idea is that you pay *us* money for the goods.' At last something interesting was happening. The huddle saw the joke and smiled.

'All right!' shouted Bernard, not the least abashed. 'You drive a hard bargain mister. I'll give you a pound for the rubbish.' The unsuccessful auctioneer threw in the towel.

'Any increase on a pound?' He waited for a moment and then he struck his clipboard with his pen and the goods belonged to Bernard. We headed back to the taxi after he'd deposited a single pound note with the clerk. I raised the subject with the now very cheerful scrap dealer.

'Will it be worth even taking away, Bernard? You'll have to send quite a few trucks to collect it, and what with the men's time, fuel and all that sort of thing you could come out a loser.' By now I was quite an authority on the economics of running a taxi, so I felt duty bound to give Bernard what advice I could. He could always change his mind and leave it to rot.

'It's been a good day,' he assured me. 'By the time the kids have separated the chrome from the steel and the tin it'll weigh in for two or three hundred quid, nae bother.' Brilliant, I thought. The man knows his trade and had run rings round all the other would-be shrewdies at the auction. If I had estimated the value properly I could have hired a lorry and if I made £100 profit it would have represented a killing to me. What Bernard said next made me feel quite sick.

'The lead, on the other hand, will fetch two or three thousand, nae bother.' Two or three thousand pounds for the lead!

'What lead?' No one had mentioned lead, and I was completely confused.

'Most of that stuff is old X-ray equipment.' Bernard explained patiently. 'Under the chrome is a layer of lead. That's why it's so heavy. In the big screens it's at least an inch thick. Aye, it's been a good day. I'd have gone as high as a grand if I'd had to, nae bother.'

On the drive back to Leith I was ecstatic with suppressed excitement. Quite by chance I had discovered the holy grail of successful buying and selling at auctions. Bernard had unwittingly let slip the secret that was simplicity itself, as all the best ideas are. Buy what no one else realises is a bargain and sell it for a huge profit.

This was going to be easy-peasy; I was on my way at last.

5

PC BERT

After completing an apprenticeship as a joiner and cabinet-maker, Bert was called up to complete his two years' national service and had served out his time in Malaya during the troubles there, to return as fit as a butcher's dog. His height, fitness and enthusiasm made him a natural for the job of policeman. Two tales from his probationary period will indicate the kind of man he was.

On hearing that a colleague, who was a few weeks from retirement, had a prisoner on his hands in a police box in the Corstorphine district, Bert, fearing for the old boy's safety, swung into action. The 'old boy' in question was a mere fifty years of age and was about to complete thirty years in the force. Bert was at Haymarket and imperiously held up his hand to stop the first car travelling in the required direction. He explained the gravity of the situation and requested a lift, and this was naturally granted. When Bert arrived at the police box and opened the door he found the old policeman sitting at ease drinking a mug of tea and enjoying a cigarette. Accepting that the prisoner had escaped, Bert demanded to know where he was headed, as he would undoubtedly recapture him in double-quick time. The old policeman patiently explained that his prisoner was jammed, out of harm's way, under the tiny desk, restrained in that position by his size-12 boots.

Another illustration of the calibre of Bert happened when he was on one of his first lone street patrols on a Wednesday afternoon in Gorgie Road. Wednesday was early closing day at that time, and although all the shops were closed, it was part of his duty to try the locks at the rear of the various shops, warehouses and office premises. In a quiet lane behind some shops as he passed an office block a window was opened and a leg appeared. As the man dropped to the ground he was grabbed by Bert and pushed against the wall. A second man followed by a third and fourth eventually arrived into his custody. Bert had only a single pair of handcuffs and four to one are not good odds for an experienced policeman, never mind a probationer, but Bert was up to the task. He had the four spreadeagled against the wall with legs apart and leaning on their finger tips while he strode up and down behind them, swinging his truncheon. Not just any truncheon, but a lead-lined one inherited from his father, who had been a country policeman. This was in the days before personal radios, and a stalemate ensued. Bert could not risk marching his prisoners away and could not move from the spot. At long last an old lady happened by that back alley and Bert was able to ask her to let the police know where he was. His duty sergeant eventually appeared and enquired as to which police force he thought he served. Did he think that he was in America? No words of commendation and no explanation of what to do with four prisoners when quite alone.

Bert was always full of fun and he and I were to enjoy many adventures. I never met anyone, apart from criminals, who ever had a bad word to say about Bert. His two years' probationary service were packed with incident and soon passed. He quite fancied CID work, but there was a waiting list, so he settled down to life as a beat policeman.

When licensed premises are broken into at night the police are particularly attentive, since there is always the possibility of a free pint of beer. On one celebrated occasion a licensed grocer's shop in Nicolson Street had been raided and Bert and his colleague from a neighbouring beat found themselves allocated the task of tidying things up. Their motorised mates had evidently better fish to fry and other beat policemen were alerted to be on the lookout for suspicious characters carrying bottles and cigarettes, and as a result many an innocent, wending his unsteady way home late that night clutching his perfectly legitimate 'cairry-oot', was accused of the dastardly deed. By the time the fingerprint team had arrived and the key-holder of the premises located it was clear that the culprits were unlikely to be apprehended, and this was good news indeed. The first prize would have been a capture, but in the circumstances there could be a consolation award. Crime in those long-forgotten days could be profitable for everyone concerned. The shopkeeper could claim for excessive and imaginary losses and the duty policeman was often treated to a packet of fags or a bottle of beer.

This time the plan must have been to swindle the insurance company of a vast amount by claiming that the thieves had used motor transport to make the raid and the few bottles taken would grow to cases in the claim. The proprietor was kindness itself and presented Bert and his beat mate with a bottle of Scotch and a quantity of cigarettes. Now anyone can justify to the duty sergeant the fact that he is carrying two packets of twenty, but a bottle takes a bit more explaining if it is not to be either confiscated or shared. I received an urgent telephone call and was given instructions to visit a particular lamppost fitted with one of the ubiquitous little white wastepaper baskets that were quite popular, as their use kept the streets in pristine condition. It was kept under observation by Bert from a discreet distance until I could arrive at the specified spot, where I found a full bottle of whisky wrapped in an old newspaper. The booty was instantly transferred to the box seat of the taxi and all of us then returned to our respective duties. A few weeks later, well after midnight, when trade had slackened off and I was looking forward to clocking off, I received a cryptic telephone call from Bert asking if I could attend at an address in Danderhall. I could and I did. Before I got to the house in question I became quite excited because outside it were parked a police van, a police car and a dog-handler's van. Clearly something big was afoot and I could be on the telephone to the *Express* or the *Mail* to claim my reward for providing first information on a crime of some sort, but I was to be sadly disappointed.

The house was the scene of a party, and the bottle of Scotch which was still under the seat of my taxi, a valued contribution. There were five policemen present in uniform, Bert in half dress and myself in mufti, but only two women. Danderhall was a mining village at that time and most of the men in the village worked ungodly hours in a night, early, day- or back-shift pattern. We needed a few of the wives whose husbands were safely underground. Women are deceivers ever, and on this occasion the ingenuity displayed was of a high order. One of the girls knocked on the door of a neighbour whose husband was fast asleep in bed beside her. She explained that one of her children had been dreadfully sick and made a mess of the sheets, blankets and pillowcases, and please could she borrow some. As the wink was tipped the neighbour insisted that she should come round to help out. Her husband was nudged awake long enough to get the message and promptly went back to dreamland while his wife went out to play. This stratagem was repeated until the proper male-to-female balance was achieved, and the party commenced. It was quite riotous as such parties go, but the noise level had to be severely curtailed. To this day I am amazed that such an event could have been successfully arranged without a rumour eventually exposing all. From reports received it was not long before every suitably available woman in the village had heard the details and insisted that if there were to be a repeat performance their door should be knocked on first.

One story told by one of the wives made me laugh. She related that she and a girlfriend had visited the next village to attend a dance and both had finished up the evening romantically involved. Naturally they used false names to protect their identities. A few days later she heard a car draw up outside her home and it looked vaguely familiar. The driver when he emerged was definitely familiar, because he was her romantic entanglement from the night of the dance. He came up the path and knocked at the door. She was having kittens in the kitchen as her husband answered the knock. The unknown caller was invited inside and introduced as her husband's workmate in the pit, and she was advised that they were going fishing together. No doubt at work her paramour would have boasted of his successful conquest at the village dance and might even have mentioned names. The use of a nom-de-plume in a mining village is an essential precaution to be taken at all times.

Spontaneous parties were a regular happening about this time, probably encouraged by the regressive licensing laws coupled with the dullness of working life. Where and when this party took place is lost from my memory bank, but I remember that it was held in the freezing depths of winter and an incident from it still makes me smile. There were many more males than females in attendance and for some reason one of the girls decided to treat the gentlemen to an impromptu striptease. It was to be a parody of the famous Dance of the Seven Veils, but veils being scarce, seven items of clothing were substituted. An ad hoc orchestra was created and the biggest section was the combs-and-paper ensemble. The tune bore a slight similarity to 'All the girls in France do the hula-hula dance', familiar to everyone. For reasons of daftness or to give the event a Middle Eastern flavour, the band wore knotted handkerchiefs on their heads. The budding Gypsy Rose Lee jumped up onto the tabletop and began her rather laborious routine. Two on-duty police officers were sitting in front-row seats hemmed close together by the crush of onlookers. I recall that my instrument was the bottle and a metal bottle-opener which, though I say it myself, I played rather well. Chinking them together to regulate the tempo was a very important function, and my secondary role was to open beer bottles as required. This was many years before the unfortunate habit of drinking from the necks of bottles became popular, and in the mêlée it was difficult to fill a glass due to the constant jostling by the excited fans.

I had just passed a couple of opened bottles to replenish the glasses of the pair of night-shift polis when the artiste became extremely daring and exposed a boob. The shouts of delight and the excitement this breathtaking action generated ensured that every head was looking up and every eye focused on the part being displayed. One of the bobbies pushed the neck of his bottle into his glass whilst still gazing aloft. His companion was nudging his arm with his elbow to draw his attention to what everyone was watching, when the bottle's neck missed the glass and entered his trousers between two fly buttons. The pressure and the nudging ensured that he was unable to remove it until every last drop of cold frothy beer had poured down his legs. The poor soul was forced to go back on duty wearing a sodden pair of trousers. Being navy blue in colour the damage did not show, but he ran a serious risk of frostbite of the willy during the rest of his night shift.

It probably served him right for skiving off duty when honest citizens expected him to be safeguarding their hearths and homes. It just goes to show what unexpected dangers lurk when there is free beer around.

6

A MODEL DENTAL NURSE

There is no doubt that if you study the youthful activities of star footballers or cricketers and dozens of other successful adults, you will doubtless discover that they have practised their craft over a number of years, however youthful they are when they hit the big time. Owen of Liverpool and Beckham of Manchester United and other top-flight stars are prime examples. It seems that as boys, or babies even, a football was attached to their booties. Tiger Woods is another former child prodigy who has swept all before him. It's the same in the arts – Yehudi Menuhin bestrode the world stage all his life. That is where I went wrong with women. I did not get in enough practice, and just when I was the right age to embark on experimentation, I was sent to the Egyptian desert for two long years where there were no women at all. I needed to play catch-up, and when I heard that there was a party to be held at one of city's 'better' addresses in a flat owned by a friend of mine, I was determined to wangle an invitation.

Drink at parties is inclined to make people bold and improve the chances of the amateur. So it was, with my taxi stashed round the corner and a clear conscience that I was simply taking a couple of hours off duty that I made my entrance. Serious drinking was out as far as I was concerned. There was nothing moral about my decision, because in those far-off days drinking and driving was commonplace. I was just not all that keen on alcohol and my preferred tipple was lager with a good dash of lime, and you'd have to down a goodly number of half-pints of that to become even merry. Others, full of booze, found it the easiest thing in the world to chat to girls who were strangers. I would invariably find myself discussing mundane rubbish with a group of males similarly afflicted and just dying to pluck up the courage to approach a female. We were male wallflowers.

There was one girl in the room who was outstandingly attractive as far as I was concerned. She was tall and slender, with brilliant teeth. I kept sneaking sly glances at her as I talked to my new friends about motorbikes. On returning from a visit to the toilet I bumped into this very comely maiden. It was actually she who collided with me, but I was more than happy to take the blame and the mutual apologies became a conversation in no time; soon I was chatting away effortlessly. Thankfully she was a good listener, and gradually my gabbling died down to a more normal rate. It was like riding a bike for the first time; you think you'll never get the hang of it and depend on someone holding the back of the saddle, but when they let go and you are not aware of the fact, you are off. Speed seems necessary if you are to keep going, but this is not so. Once you achieve balance you can slow down and execute all sorts of figures of eight, swerves and even slow time when you have to waggle the handlebars to keep upright. So it was with Fiona, and once I started talking slowly it was plain sailing.

I discovered that she was a dental nurse but harboured ambitions to become a model. At the time, to be described as a model was something of a compliment and not a reference to someone who took their clothes off, but rather put them on. She had every attribute that was required to become a mannequin. Tall and slim and graceful, coiffured elegantly, and with a smile designed to draw attention to those perfect teeth. I told her that I thought that *Vogue* magazine would only need to see her photograph and her future would be assured, and it seemed the right thing to say. After a few more pleasantries she took my hand and whispered. 'Come with me, I want to show you something.' It was not an order, but it was compelling. Probably this was the voice she used when escorting patients to the chairside.

I was led down a short passageway to a bedroom where the centrepiece was a big double bed with a motorist's 'L' plate suspended from the footboard. I was looking around for photographs of Fiona or a photo album, because I was sure that was the purpose of our visit. As far as I knew it could be her flat. But when I turned round to look at her, she was neatly folding her dress over a chair back, and was standing in stockings and suspenders, a brassière with matching tiny panties and a string of pearls with pearl-drop earrings – and nothing else. She immediately jumped into bed. I admit I was green and a young man without experience, but I'm not daft either. Before she had time to pull the bedclothes up to her chin my clobber was all over the floor and I was in beside her wearing my new 'Y' fronts, which were then quite a fashion statement. I honestly cannot remember whether or not I kept my socks on, but I probably did. This was a dream suddenly come true. I was as sober as the proverbial legal gentleman and I'm sure that Fiona was too.

For want of anything else to do we cuddled while the bed warmed up. I warmed up much faster than the bed did and Fiona assisted me out of my underpants. She did not appear over keen to assist my first moves, but after a great deal of amateurish fumbling behind her back I managed to remove her bra. To my surprise most of her bust departed with this piece of frothy lingerie. I was to discover to my delight that a relatively flat chest has a charm all of its own. Removing her panties was a finger-shaking, heart-thumping joy. Those long, long legs were a journey of exploration on their own and then the kissing and cuddling and mutual caressing began. There was no need to rush, as Fiona kept reminding me. I was anxious that she should have no inkling that I was a kindergarten student trying for university entrance exam success. The door burst open and instead of a blackmailing photographer it was simply someone asking if we would like our drinks replenished.

I would love to report that I played Fiona's body like a musical instrument, but I can't tell a lie. We touched and stroked, rubbed and squeezed, and before long it was clear that there was no possible chance of anything more with the lovely dental nurse. No wonder, as the door opened five times in all. Twice more offering to freshen up our drinks, and once with sincere apologies for disturbing us, and lastly by a couple with a complaint – had we not finished yet, as they were waiting their turn to use the preheated bed? No wonder Fiona was only prepared to tolerate slap-and-tickle under such public conditions. It was agreed that I would drive her home at the end of the evening, and we rejoined the other guests. Fiona suggested that we mingle, and we moved off in separate directions, she to enjoy the laughter and banter of the party, and me to curse the slowness of the passage of time with my bunch of wallflowers. I told them nothing, and it is doubtful that I would have been believed anyway.

There was, however, a peculiar incident when a large chap, clearly from the Highlands or Islands from his accent and a complete stranger to me, approached and asked how I had got on with the delightful dentist's helper.

'Wass it yourself that wass in the bedroom with that good-looking woman?' he enquired in his soft Highland burr. 'I wass sure it wass you.' I held up my hands, metaphorically speaking, and admitted that he was right.

'Did she take off all her clothes?' was his next question. That he knew her employment troubled me slightly and I assumed that he was a former boyfriend. They must have broken up, and to prove how easy it was for her to replace him, she had picked the nearest bloke and dragged him to the bedroom. Rubbing the nose of an ex in it is not a good strategy as it can very easily lead to fisticuffs. For the delightful Fiona I was prepared to chance my arm, but I was completely wrong.

'She iss a lovely girl right enough, but she iss a queer one, so she iss.' He was on the button there. I asked if he was the ex-husband or boyfriend, but he quickly put me right. 'I neffer saw her before last week, when she took me to bed, but nothing at all happened. She iss a right queer one, so she iss. I think she iss a Lesbian.' If Fiona was a Lesbian I was going to put them on my shopping list, because for a beginner like me she was a load of fun, and I had the drive home to look forward to. Hugh, for that turned out to be his name, was unrelenting in his cross-examination. 'Do you think she iss on the game and wants you to offer her money once you are excited?' There was no answer to that, but if it had been the case surely she would have hinted about how hard-up she was at some stage. Hugh was a disappointed man. For a week he had been in the throes of a full-blown romance, at least in his head, and had thought that when he turned up this week the lovely leggy Fiona would consummate their mutual passion. Instead she had cut him dead.

I knew the feeling. After a pen-pal romance of some two and a half years in the RAF when I was sitting in my little tent in the desert I had received a 'Dear John' letter from my dark and dimpled Liverpool lovely. The relationship had been chaste, but it still hurt, and I had vowed that I would never fall in love again. But things change, and I have to admit that my head was filled with the images of Fiona and memories of our bedroom antics. The scent of her perfume and the exciting animal smell of her sweat when aroused were unforgettable. Her long, long legs and that . . . I had not been this excited since the school dance nine years before, when, as a spotty and gawky 14-year-old, I had walked in a trance from Bruntsfield to Saughtonhall escorting a pork butcher's daughter. Her curves were a credit to her father's occupation, coupled with her natural puppy fat. We were all severely rationed for meat, but he must have managed to take the odd cut home with him. I was her fourth choice of escort from the dance, but the single kiss she bestowed on me when parting allowed me to float back home to Marchmont without effort. Things were different now, and some unimaginable delights were in store for me, but until then I would play it cool.

At last we made our way to the taxi and I set off to drive Fiona to her home, which naturally enough was miles away, up the Lanark Road. When we got there it was late and Saturday was a working day at the surgery, with an eight-thirty start. The separation of me being in the front seat and she in the rear, sitting all alone, did nothing to encourage closeness, and the fact that my vehicle turned out to be a taxi may have disappointed her. We parted with no more than a perfunctory peck on the cheek, but there was another party scheduled to take place seven days hence and I would see her there.

I fidgeted for a whole week, but time soon passes when you are kept busy. At last the night of the party arrived and Fiona was already there when I arrived, but she seemed a bit distant, and I put it down to her disappointment in discovering my profession. In her daily world dashing dentists would be her workmates and she probably planned to marry one in the future if her modelling career failed to take off. I waited patiently. She ignored me completely, and later I saw her slip out of the room, hand in hand with a guy who obviously thought that Christmas had come early. An hour later Hugh and I cornered the slightly embarrassed chap.

'How did you get on with that gorgeous girl?' we chorused in unison.

'Fabulous,' he boasted. 'What a goer. I was glad to get back to the party. She's a nymphomaniac. Can't get enough.' Together we politely challenged him.

'You're a lying bastard.' He looked shocked. 'Is there a two-way mirror in there? How did you know?' He then confessed all and joined the ranks of the frustrated Fiona fanciers.

Either she made it right to the top as a clothes-horse or settled down to domesticity with a successful dental practice attached. With her fearsome self-control, whatever she chose to do, I'm sure that the decision was hers and hers alone.

7

PEDRO THE PIRATE

Pedro, due to his criminal record, couldn't qualify to drive a legal taxi so he became a pirate operator. Most pirate cab drivers kept their activities low key. Every client they carried was supposed to book in advance, in order to be legitimate, but this rule was normally ignored. To be caught breaking it could invalidate their passenger accident insurance, if they had any, in the event of a pile-up. This is as true today as it was then. Pirates often had a discreet arrangement with a few public houses to provide service for their clients without advance notice, but this was hardly a hanging offence. If in the course of their duties they saw people waiting for taxis outside a cinema or theatre they would slip in and pick them up.

There was little we could do about that, but Pedro was much bolder than the average corsair. He would brazenly park his car as if on a rank in busy parts of the town. When his clients complained to the cab office police inspector that a cab without a meter had picked them up and demanded a ridiculous fare, the police inspector would shrug his shoulders and deny that it was within his jurisdiction. The trade heartily disliked Pedro the Pirate almost as much as they loathed the cab inspector.

To augment his income Pedro pimped off his wife, and a few neighbourhood housewives and friends who were on the game on a part-time basis, drove housebreakers to and from their targets and generally behaved in an antisocial way. He and his car were far from discreet. His old Austin 16 was fitted with white-wall tyres making it instantly recognisable. He dressed in a similarly garish fashion. When Rabbie Burns said that it would be a good idea if we could see ourselves through other people's eyes he knew what he was on about.

Pedro was convinced that he was a second Al Capone, and dressed with that in mind. His hair, most of it thankfully hidden beneath a Panama hat, was jet black and greasy, and so long that it fell below his collar at the back. Even Teddy boys at that time, who sported the famous DA cut, had clean necks, but Pedro was a soap-dodger. He wore a pencil-slim Robert Coleman moustache, and he was overweight, but concealed it well by wearing baggy and out-of-date zoot suits. His shoulders were well padded, and on his podgy fingers he wore so many chunky silver rings that they could have served as knuckledusters if Pedro had been a bit more of a hero. His *pièce de résistance*, which made his appearance unique, were his two-tone shoes. Depending on that day's sartorial ensemble they would be black and white or brown and white. We wondered where he got them, but with hindsight they were probably golfing shoes with the studs removed. He thought that he epitomised the all-American look and that with luck he could pass for a gangster in a B-movie. We thought that he looked the cheap spiv that he was. His regular hangout was Eddie Carson's late-night rendezvous on Leith Walk.

Although some would still consider me a rookie, I had by now passed the 'knowledge' and left Jock and his pirate fleet behind. Paul had been as good as his word and offered me a full-time driving job. He was a paid-up member of City Cabs, and that group of drivers had bought the exclusive rights to provide taxis for the three railway stations in Edinburgh. I was looking forward to the luxury of a steady stream of clients from this source, but Paul, in his wisdom, decided to switch to Radio Cabs, a rival group where he was sure additional night work could be found now that we were double-shifting in his Beardmore.

This was my last night of seven straight 12-hour night shifts. I was due for a 24-hour break before starting seven day shifts. At least half my rest day would be spent in sleep, but the rest would be like a holiday. In a hundred years' time people will marvel at the long hours we worked, and the poor conditions we worked under. We could become Oliver Twists, in the minds of twenty-first-century citizens, with filmmakers clamouring for the rights to expose the cruelty we suffered.

I still had one night to get through and I had been busy shuttling about from the ten o'clock pub closing time. I picked up a man and two women who asked me where they could find Pedro. The man looked a bit of a hard case. He was over six feet tall, and muscular, and the women looked a bit tarty, and just Pedro's type. The blonde was tall and slim and the dark-haired girl was smaller and rounder. I explained that he would probably be busy with his personal trade, but that he would be sure to turn up at Eddie's café at some time, and it was agreed that I would take them there. They were not at all chatty, and we drove to Leith Walk in silence. Pedro's ostentatious taxi was parked outside the café and I pointed it out.

'There's his car, he'll be inside.' It was now that I got a good look at my passengers. He spoke with the trace of a local accent but the blue marks on his face looked to me like a coal miner's scars. He was well built and spare and not a man to cross, I thought. The women were complete opposites. One was certainly English and the other definitely Scottish and local. The Scot was the tall cool blonde of the brittle variety. The smaller, dark-haired one was English and more solid than plump. She was the wife of the big man and looked capable of digging coal alongside him.

'Could you tell Pedro that we'd like to see him?' I was parked about 30 yards from the caff, but, being a rookie, I trotted off to oblige my fares. They could have been looking for part-time work, with the quiet man as a minder, but it was none of my business. When I pushed open the door of the café I raised my voice.

'Pedro!' I shouted above the clamour, 'I've got a bloke and a couple of birds in the car and they say that they want to see you.'

He thought that his ship had come in. In his phoney American accent he acknowledged me.

'Ho-kay, do-kay, I be wid you in a minute.' Not bad for a local boy born in the shadow of Easter Road football ground. I returned to the taxi and told the trio that he would be out in a minute to see them. The blonde slipped out of the cab as Pedro emerged from the café, mounted the steps up to pavement level, and began to walk up the broad expanse of concrete towards my taxi. At that moment the cool blonde came to the boil. She rushed at the luckless pirate with arms flailing in an attempt to beat him about the head. She was screaming at the top of her voice.

'You got my Si done, you bastard, and I'll do for you.' It was all very dramatic. Her attack on Pedro was unsuccessful because he proved that under pressure he could move his bulk faster than he could talk and he darted back into the café in full retreat. My other two passengers had chased after the boiling blonde and were leading her back to the cab when Pedro and a gang of six buccaneers burst out of the café and advanced towards us. Pedro, a step behind the other six, was obviously annoyed. He clearly did not fancy his chances against the blonde in a one-on-one, and he was mouthing at me and pointing a finger. His American accent had deserted him in his distress.

'See him,' he screamed out loudly, 'That's him, he's the finger man.' I was now definitely one of Pedro's enemies, albeit unwillingly. The battle lines were drawn. One hard case, two women and a coward against seven heavies. At that precise moment a friend of mine, seeing the commotion and recognising the duffel coat, stopped his MG roadster to see what was happening. He wandered across, completely oblivious to the tense situation, and asked me how I was getting on. The odds had changed dramatically. One hard case, two women and a coward and one bewildered innocent, versus seven now none-too-confident heavies. The odds of seven to five were not good enough for Pedro, who led his troops, like the Grand Old Duke of York, down the hill again. Their rearguard action was mainly verbal and aimed at me.

I drove my fares to their home and was invited inside for drinks and a proper introduction. He was Michael and his wife was Mary; Michael's sister Marjorie, always known as Marge, was now not only tall but cool again. After the tension in Leith Street we were all much more relaxed by now and Michael proffered some information on the background to the affray. He went into an old routine to introduce his wife Mary. 'We met at the dancing at the army camp I was in and I fancied her like mad. When I asked her for a dance I said to her, "My name's Michael but I'm no a Si, Si, Si, Saint!" And she said, "My name's Mary and I'm no a Vi, Vi, Vi, very good dancer."' They fell about laughing at the hundredth telling of the old chestnut. Michael had married Mary and they had settled in the south. Only recently, following the death of Mary's mother, had they decided to up sticks to Edinburgh for a change of scene.

Marge, still simmering at her inability to avenge her husband's incarceration, was not amused. Her husband Si, or more properly Simon, was supping porridge in a prison in the far north of Scotland.

That he was in jail because he deserved to be there was not the point, it was how he came to be caught that was the problem. Pedro had been retained as the driver for a break-in at Blyth's Stores at Tollcross and everything had gone according to plan. The loot was mainly cash. Pedro thought that now that the contract had been successfully completed his fee should be increased. Simon had pointed out, not unreasonably, that if they had come away empty-handed Pedro would still have expected and received his fare. That they had landed the spoils was the luck of the draw, and if he had been keen on a full share he should have joined them inside the store. Risk was not Pedro's business and he explained this to Simon, which may have been a lapse of judgement, since Simon had a fearsome reputation as a violent hoodlum. Knowledge is power, and Si warned Pedro of the likely consequences if Pedro was daft enough to grass him up. A stalemate ensued.

Pedro reverted to type, he couldn't stop himself. He told the police who the culprits were. They already knew, but were still short of proof – the sort of proof that would stand up in court and be accepted as beyond all reasonable doubt was hard to come by.

Edinburgh has a world-famous university, but very few realise just how many of its hundreds of departments carry out original research in a wide range of disciplines. At this time there was a breakthrough in jurisprudence that went unannounced. The police, however, used the new skill to convict poor Simon. It was the ability to transfer a fingerprint from one surface and site to another. Surprise, surprise, part of a fingerprint was found on the glass panel of a door in Blyth's and it matched one of Simon's prints already on file at police headquarters. This damning piece of evidence sent him down for three years of lumpy porridge. Simon's complaint was that he had never removed his gloves during the robbery since he always wore two pairs; leather ones over surgical rubber ones, but it hardly constituted an acceptable defence. This taught the bold Simon, and everyone else who heard his story, a valuable lesson. If the plod is after you they will get you eventually.

On release he continued his criminal ways, but this time wearing a white collar. He turned to any lucrative criminal activity that did not actually require him to break and enter. He never again put himself at risk of imprisonment but made oodles of cash in his new career. He still had his muscles and willingness to batter into submission anyone who crossed him or his criminal associates. His firm prospered.

A few years afterwards, in the USA, it was heralded as a breakthrough in technique when it was acknowledged that it was now possible to transfer fingerprints from one site to another. The Edinburgh police beat them to it by years.

I had to get on with my work, but Michael extended an open invitation to call again at any time, insisting that I would always be welcome. I finished my shift and handed the duffel coat and the Beardmore over to Paul and went home to bed. But that was not to be the end of the matter.

8

THE NAAFI

Thinking-time is the one thing every cabbie has in abundance, and since my visit to the auction with Bernard I'd been turning over in my mind the things that I had learned. It all seemed so simple. Buy cheap – the obvious place to do that was at auction – and sell on for a reasonable profit. Don't be too greedy; better to turn your money over several times and make more that way rather than trying to make a killing on every purchase. The cheaper that you can sell the stuff the sooner someone will buy it. Anything will sell if it's cheap enough – well, nearly anything.

Another sale of government surplus had been advertised at the same venue as before and it was pencilled into my diary. Due to the pressures of work I didn't manage to get a copy of the catalogue, but I was sure there would be bargains galore. I would take Bernard's advice and turn a few pounds' profit, 'nae bother'. Deciding what to bid for without the catalogue would be difficult, but I had an instinct in such matters and it rarely let me down. Cab driving could become a mere hobby when my main income came from dealing. Pouncing on undetected bargains and reaping the just rewards would be a pleasant way to pass the time. Later on I would probably need a warehouse and a yard to store bigger items and larger quantities. Luck did not come into it; just common sense, the ability to see value where others did not. I could hardly wait for the day of the auction.

For a taxi driver to pass a raised hand, particularly when his 'for hire' flag is up, is well-nigh impossible, or it was for me at any rate. Every time I set off for the sale I was ambushed by prospective passengers. They always wanted to travel in the opposite direction from the auction but the old bird-in-the-hand syndrome is one I find difficult to ignore. On other days I could travel miles with my hire light on and find no takers. Naturally, because it was the day of the auction I was inundated with work. No one was interested in going towards Fairmilehead; anywhere else was fine but not towards the south of the city. By mid-afternoon I had actually managed to make it as far as the field being used for parking when someone who had been to the auction and was leaving hailed me for a trip back to town. On the way to the city centre I asked him how it was going.

'It's a give-away day. Not many people have turned up and those who have seem to have no money.' It was my day; deep down I just knew it, and I was going to that sale if the queen herself tried to hail my cab. As he dismounted from the taxi my passenger threw a catalogue into a deep puddle. It was an omen. I retrieved the booklet, which was sodden and unreadable. The inner voice told me I had to attend this sale.

At last I was standing among the sparse and apparently penurious crowd as the final few items came under the hammer. It was the same auctioneer as the previous sale and he was having difficulty coaxing bids for the penultimate lot.

'Come along gentlemen, who'll give me a start on these superlative items? Two gross to each case. You'll never find better quality anywhere. These were specially commissioned by the NAAFI during the war from a nationally renowned china-clay manufacturer in the Potteries. Made to their own specification, you'll not find cups like them anywhere. They're finished in a snow-white high gloss that would grace any table. By the way, there's no lettering on them to indicate that they were NAAFI ware. Nothing printed on them whatever. Now come along. Who'll start me off?' Who needs a catalogue with a description like that? Apart from a fidgeting of feet there was no response from his audience.

'Come along,' pleaded the auctioneer, 'Who'll give me a start?' Nobody responded. 'Right,' he said. 'I'll tell you what I'll do; I'll sell them in case lots if that will help. Each tea-chest contains two gross. That way you can share them among friends and family. Shall we say ten pounds?' Apparently not on this occasion, but he pressed on regardless. 'OK, what about five?' He said it but no one agreed with him. 'Can I hear five to set me off?' He listened in vain. This could be just the item that I was after. I might have to buy the saucers and plates separately so that when combined into eighteen-piece tea sets they would sell like hot cakes. I was sorely tempted to open the bidding. The auctioneer was nothing if not persistent. 'Can I have a bid or do I withdraw them from the sale?' This was an alarming prospect so I decided to emulate Bernard and take a chance.

'I'll give you a pound.' My nerve failed me when it came to the 'to take them away' bit. There was a moment of silence.

'I'm bid a pound, who'll give me two?' queried the man on the box, looking round in an anxious manner. 'Two? Two pounds? Two pounds, anywhere?' There were no takers and he struck his clipboard with his pen and announced. 'Sold to the gentleman at the back.' I had made my first swoop as a dealer. 'How many cases do you want, sir?' The gentleman at the back only pondered for a second when common sense kicked in.

'How many have you got?' I was cool. 'Six.' Then I heard a voice remarkably like mine say, 'I'll take the lot.' From the awed glances I was getting from the crowd it was clear that they were impressed by my slick *modus operandi*. They knew a shrewd buyer when they saw one, and it was clear that none of them had thought of buying the sets in their component parts and linking them up.

I had done it and I was on my way. The taxi could hold only three tea-chests at a time. One box was stored in the open-sided luggage bay, and two more with much difficulty, and some paint scraping, in the back. Running true to form, now that the taxi was full of merchandise and off call, passengers seemed to queue up to hail me at every stage of my journey home. After a second run and a great deal of effort, skinned knuckles and much puffing and panting, the six tea-chests were home at last.

I installed them in what might laughingly be referred to as a potting shed at the bottom of what no botanist would recognise as the garden. How many was a dozen gross? The answer is 'a lot'. I used a jemmy to force the lid off one of the chests so that I could admire my purchase. Fumbling in the straw I pulled out a cup. A very peculiar cup, and one that was large enough to hold more than a pint of liquid. It was snow-white and seemed to weigh a ton. The clay was at least a quarter of an inch thick but for some reason the handle was missing. On turning it over I discovered that inside the bottom rim it was clearly embossed 'NAAFI property'. Nowhere could I see any marks to indicate where the handle had been affixed. I laid it on top of the box and quickly fumbled inside for a second one. As I did this I knocked the first cup and it tipped over and rolled off the top of the box, fell fully four feet to the concrete floor – and bounced. The second cup was also minus a handle, as were all the others. Every single one of them was *sans* a handle. I had bought 1,728 ugly heavy cups without handles. But we entrepreneurs love a challenge.

My first executive decision was to forget about trying to buy saucers and plates to match the handle-less cups. This was just as well because none had ever been manufactured. I had been guilty of making an error of judgement and could have bought all six cases for a single pound had I been more experienced. Seeing the goods before bidding would have helped too. Within the next month I became an authority on the china clay industry. Had it been possible to design handles, they could not be attached so long after firing. My cups would have to be sold as they were. My first sale was to the Greyfriars Hotel in the Grassmarket. This grandly named residence was for the lower end of the homeless market, where the residents had a habit of stealing the cutlery and crockery. The management bought four dozen as a trial at sixpence each. The experiment was a failure. The ungrateful itinerants, and other clients of the doss-house, went on strike, claiming that the free tea in the cups burned their fingers. They were not the only ones who had fingers burned and I was forced to repossess them. Some fun-fair folk thought that the cups would be suitable for throwing wooden balls at, but alas! they would not break. They suggested that I call again when I had a supply of plates. It appeared that the special specification demanded by the NAAFI was reinforced concrete.

At last I had a breakthrough when I came across a youthful baker setting up business on Young Street who thought them ideal for baking his individual steamed puddings. He bought three dozen on the spot and warned me to be on standby, since he expected that the fierce heat of the ovens would break them on a regular basis, and he would need a repeat order each month. I had discovered the right price at sixpence each, and although the return might be slow it would be steady. I had got rid of three dozen and managed to get back eighteen shillings of my six pound investment. I did not charge for sales costs or carriage. Alas, the cups were too good. The baker reported that despite being roasted, cooled and even kept in a freezer on a daily basis, not a single cup broke or even developed a hairline crack. In fact, they looked good for several years of wear. I was at my wits' end and anxious not to let the world know what an ass I had been. This meant that I could ask only trusted friends for advice.

I would like to offer a prize to any reader who can come up with a suitable use for such objects. In the end I got rid of every one of them in one fell swoop. It was not profitable, but by then it did not matter as I had written off the financial loss, putting it down to hard-earned experience. How did I do it?

I moved house and left them in the potting shed, my posh name for the old disused toilet at the bottom of the back garden.

9

THE TRIFFIDS

Some bright spark in the City Chambers had the idea that Edinburgh would benefit from the introduction of traffic wardens, that rare breed of men and women drawn from all walks of life who were destined to become universally unloved once they put on the uniform to carry out their duties. They were mainly recruited from among those who would have dearly loved to become policemen and policewomen but in some way lacked the qualifications essential to recruitment. Education, age, sex, height, eyesight; the list is long. At the same time as the wardens were recruited, it was thought essential to introduce parking meters to raise the funds to pay their wages. It was confidently predicted that the cost of the installation of the actual meters would easily be raised from the motoring public, and of course the prediction was accurate. The meters raised enough money to subsidise an extravagant city council. Naturally enough, motorists would need to be herded in the direction of the meters by the designation of 'no parking' zones signified by single and double yellow lines. Foresighted folk who bought shares in yellow-paint-producing factories did very well. Hardly a day passed when the yellow tide failed to claim more territory and the accompanying parking meters sprang up, triffid-like, overnight, frightening the life out of the residents. We who drove taxis were content that the regulations did not apply to us.

A fare had asked me to wait for him in George Street, and I was sitting minding my own business when a voice whispered in my ear. 'You'll not be waiting there for long if you don't want me to be dishing out a ticket.' I recognised the voice instantly. It belonged to Hugh. Hugh was from the far north, where he had been a boatman, fisherman, postman, joiner and undertaker, all at the same time. He was of mature years and had decided, as they do on the islands, that he wanted to get married before he turned 40. He had, I discovered, worked as a joiner for my friend the Colonel, who rented out student flats. I had seen him around at various parties. He had been a fellow sufferer whose hopes had been raised and dashed by the delightful, but strangely unattainable, Fiona. On recognising me, Hugh became much less officious. He placed his size-12 boot on the running board and settled down to pass the time.

'What do you t'ink of my new chob?' He queried. I was non-committal. 'Man, it iss chust the best chob a man could have. Walking about in God's good fresh air, meeting lots of girls in shops and offices, and getting given cups of tea everywhere. And the boots and the uniform, it iss all provided free. If I had of known that chobs like this wass to be had in Edinburgh I would haff left home years ago.' Hugh's discourse was cut short by his companion. They operated in pairs for mutual protection. 'This taxi man is a personal friend of mine,' Hugh informed him. 'You chust go on and book a few motors and I'll be with you shortly.' There was no badge of rank on Hugh's sleeve, but being the bigger man he naturally led his more fearful colleague. 'As I was saying it iss a grand chob Doogie, and I am fine and fresh for doing the Colonel's choinering at night. Your friend does not pay very well but he pays me cash in hand, and lets me have a free flat, so between the two chobs I am doing chust fine. You meet a lot of women on this chob. It iss the uniform you know.' I did know and was quite sure that Hugh would push his new-found authority to the limit if occasion or opportunity warranted it. He added a new topic. 'When you are done with your uniform, you get a new one every year you know. I can sell the old one to crofters and the like. They are fine and warm for the tractor driving.' Hugh obviously liked three sources of income. He then, to my surprise, had a gentle dig at me.

'Man, you missed a grand party the other week.' It was true that I had missed a great many festive functions recently due to the demands of keeping a cab on the road. 'I got off with a woman and took her back to my flat and found out a new technique that works a treat with them.' Now Hugh had my interest because I was in need of guidance in dealing with the fair sex. 'You must try it, man; it works every time with every woman. What you do is take the girl to your flat, but you must prepare in advance before you take her there.' I knew that Hugh's flat would be tiny, a single room in fact, and understood that it would be extremely cramped at the best of times.

'What you do,' Hugh stressed with great earnestness, 'iss to put books or something on the chair and make sure the only place for her to sit down is on the bed. Then sit down beside her. You could even give her a drink or something.' Hugh was being tainted with our city ways.

'Got you so far Hugh, what next?' He really had my attention now.

'You chust blow in her ear. It works like a charm and they chust can't resist. When she falls back on the bed you take your chance. It iss as easy as pie. You chust blow in their ears.' I had a delicious fantasy of Hugh with his cheeks bulging out as he delivered a hurricane-force wind into some unfortunate girl's ear. Her hair would be streaming out horizontally and she would be clinging to the bed for dear life. Hugh took my smile as an encouraging sign. 'Why Doogie man, until you try it you can have no idea of how well it works.' This raised a question.

'So your sex life is OK, Hugh?' He beamed a self-satisfied smile.

'Man, it iss chust fine. I am going with a Liberian girl at the moment and I think I might take her home to meet the family. She iss a lovely girl.' I had only a vague notion of where Liberia was located. I knew it was in Africa and had been created by former slaves from the United States, but that was about it. How a black girl would go down on the island was anyone's guess, but for Hugh to consider taking her home was as good as becoming engaged.

'She's coloured then, Hugh? It's a big step to take. How do you think the family will react when they meet her?' Hugh looked at me as if I had lost my marbles.

'What do you mean, coloured? She iss as white as you or me.'

I put him right. 'You said she was a Liberian, Hugh, so naturally I thought . . .' I broke off as Hugh interrupted me.

'She iss a Liberian, that iss her chob, she gives out the books in the libery on the George IV Bridge.'

10

FAROUK

Our Farouk, when he wore sunglasses, was a doppelgänger for the infamous former King of Egypt at his ripest. Over six feet tall and weighing twenty-six stones if he weighed an ounce, from a distance he actually looked shorter than he was, due to his girth. He was a very greedy man in every sense. When he and Fat Tony had their legendary set-to in the Caledonian Station over an unpaid gambling debt, they fought non-stop for more than three minutes. Belly to belly they flailed away, but neither contestant landed a blow on his opponent due to the size of their stomachs. Their arms were just too short to reach the chin of the other. It ended in a double knockdown when both collapsed due to short-ness of breath and a real prospect of a double coronary arrest.

Farouk was not a licensed taxi operator but drove an ancient boneshaker that exuded blue smoke from every aperture. He used second-hand engine oil given to him for free by various garages as an alternative to them having to pay to dispose of it. His passion was poker playing and only when his run of luck, or his sleight of hand, had deserted him, would he venture out into the streets to try to poach a few illegal passengers. His cab was not taxed or insured, so his fund-raising forays were always con-ducted at dead of night. As soon as he had collected enough to allow him to regain his place at the table his cab was abandoned until the next emergency arose.

His origins were meant to be a mystery, but anyone who read the Sunday papers and had a memory span of a year, should have been able to identify him immediately. He had been employed as a warder in a prison in Glasgow, where he augmented his official earnings by carrying contraband to the inmates from their loved ones. His nature was such that he was never satisfied. In addition to the extortionate prices that he charged the wives and families for making the lives of his charges a little more pleasant, he demanded, and received, bedroom services. Word inevitably got out when on visiting days the inmates received complaints from their nearest and dearest. A snare was laid and Farouk blundered into it. The authorities were disappointed enough to award him twelve months among his former detainees and he found out for himself what it felt like to have a lock turned behind him. There was no future for him in Glasgow, so he came to Edinburgh to try his luck.

In a way he was a genius, an evil one for sure, but a genius nevertheless. He discovered that a person is exactly what people take him to be. He had worked at creating a new image and spoke with what we used to refer to as a cut-glass accent. He could appear to be charming and dressed well when he could get his hands on any money. Whose money it was did not matter because he reasoned that if it passed through his hands it was his. He was determined to get to the top, and since the fear of prison and public exposure were no longer a threat to him, he was a dangerous man indeed.

The buzz went round that Farouk had shirts for sale and if you wanted some you had best be quick. Edinburgh in the mid to late 1950s was a monochrome place. Looking back, it was like an old black and white movie compared to the Technicolor of today. Cars were mostly painted black; buildings were soot-encrusted, clothing charcoal-grey or black. The only splash of colour was the maroon and cream of the tramcars and buses. Edinburgh was a grey city. One bright spot was Farouk's new business premises sited just off Morrison Street. It was a hive of industry, and clearly successful.

Farouk's stock of shirts was bright and cheerful. Dark red, dark green, bright pink, blue or yellow – all the colours of a rainbow, in fact a painter's palette of colours. None were available in white and very few in cream. Not everyone knows that sweets were still rationed at that time, and coupons were required to buy clothing. The enterprising Farouk ignored the need for coupons but reintroduced the wartime practice of shirt rationing. Not that they were scarce, far from it, but these were new, and in vibrant London colours. The overwhelming demand was for white shirts, but there were none. Sizes ranged from fourteen- to twenty-inch necks and all were the same price, with a minimum order of six. Three dark colours and three lighter ones, all to the Scottish eye a bit fancy and not what we would buy for ourselves, but they were cheap. Farouk could afford to be generous because he had no intention of paying for the merchandise.

Inside the premises paint brushes and ladders, rolls of wallpaper and the paraphernalia needed to open up a new shop were much in evidence. Piled from floor to ceiling were dozens and dozens of packing cases full of shirts. In police parlance, this business was a long firm fraud. The first few invoices were supplied on a 'cash with order' basis. Trouble with the decorators meant a delay in the grand opening. The eager shirt salesman pushed more stock, particularly stock that was slow-selling elsewhere, on to the 'gullible' owner. Bingo was called soon after. Overnight the stock, the decorators' gear, everything, was gone except the empty packing cases. The shop? It had been empty for so long that when these strangers showed interest the owners had been happy to give access for measuring and pre-opening purposes as the lease was due to be signed any day now.

Farouk was in funds and able to pay for the expensive clothes that had so impressed the London salesmen. He would now move on to bigger and better deals. We, wearing our brightly coloured, collar-attached shirts, would watch his progress with interest. Naturally, he disappeared from the Edinburgh scene for a time, although he had never signed an order or even allowed himself to be identified as the ringleader of the new business that had shown so much promise. He had merely been the manager. No one was ever charged in connection with the fraud, and the greedy people in far-off London presumably put it down to experience and a lesson hard-learned. For Farouk it provided the seed corn for future enterprises. Where he disappeared to was never discovered, but he clearly husbanded his new-found wealth with an eye to the future. When he reappeared he had transformed himself into a gentleman of some consequence. Some said that he had met and married a rich lady in the north of Scotland, and she had been impressed by his open handedness and charm.

It seems ironic that Farouk never wore any of the shirts that passed through his podgy hands. He was just too big. His plans for the future were big too.

11

PEDRO'S REVENGE

It was a week after my altercation with Pedro the Pirate at Eddie Carson's café and I was waiting in line at the Tollcross rank when I was approached by two very large gentlemen in identical coats and hats. Both had large feet and were unmistakably plain-clothes plod.

'What can I do for you gentlemen?' I asked in a most civil manner.

'We've had a complaint about a very serious assault.' They looked at me with distrustful eyes. 'We believe you were involved.'

'Hold on a cotton-picking minute.' Just why I used such a ridiculous greeting I have no idea, but the expression must have been in vogue at that time. It might also have been an attempt to lighten the situation because I was worried, since, with a few honourable exceptions, I don't altogether trust the plod. 'I don't know what you're talking about.' They made it crystal clear what they were talking about but did not refer to Pedro as Pedro, calling him instead by a Latin-sounding name that I had never heard before.

'Do you mean Pedro?'

'Yes,' said the second plod. 'There was an attempted razor-slashing incident the other night and you were involved.'

'What do you mean a razor-slashing? You must be joking; you've got it all wrong. A fare of mine, probably one of Pedro's girls, tried to slap his face, that's all.'

'No, no,' said number one, having his pennyworth. 'It was definitely a razor that was used.' It was quite strange that both of them should be presenting the case for the prosecution, since the normal method of interrogation was good cop, bad cop. I shook my head in disbelief and it must have had some effect.

'Listen,' I said. 'I was there, fair enough, but you were not, so I know what happened. It was simply a slap on his face.'

'Could it have been a nail file then, or the tail of a steel comb?'

'I've told you,' I repeated. 'It was definitely an open hand and she missed anyway.' The plods looked at each other, wondering what to say next. After a few minutes of deep concentration they had the answer.

'You were their get-away driver. Where did you drop them off?'

'Get-away!' I laughed out loud. 'Get-away yourselves. You're both talking nonsense and you know it. It's Pedro you're talking about. If you must know, I dropped my fares in Princes Street and I had never seen them before.'

The two men with large feet had run out of options so they satisfied themselves with warning me to 'watch it' and they wandered off. I promptly forgot all about it. Two nights later Paul was not a happy man when he handed over to me in the early dawn. He was clearly worried about something and was in fact quite aggressive towards me. If he was going to accuse me of running without the flag down he was on a non-starter because I would not diddle him out of a penny. I was not guilty either of sloping off to the pictures or any other dodge that I could think of.

'What did you get up to the other night?' he demanded. 'I very nearly copped it because of you.' It would take a lot for Paul to be worried. He was short but tough as teak, and had been driving cabs ever since he'd left the army after the war. It took a lot to get him excited. What on earth had I done? I had checked the oil and water and handed the cab over with a full tank of fuel. It was beyond me.

'What's up Paul? What am I supposed to have done?'

'Last night,' he began, 'I was driving along Corstorphine Road when I was forced into the kerb by a black Austin-16 hire car.' I had a germ of an idea of what he was about to say. 'Six blokes jumped out with iron bars in their hands set on doing over both the cab and me. It was a bit hairy I can tell you. They kept on about knowing it was me they were after because of the duffel coat. I had a narrow squeak.' Paul must have known that the Austin belonged to Pedro and I was surprised that it had only taken six of them to worry Paul. Charming and pleasant on the outside he was, but the whole trade knew that you could never best him. He would always bounce back for more until you were exhausted. He was my mentor, friend, employer and instructor, and he felt that I was his responsibility. If he was worried by the incident then I should be terrified, and I was. Driving a taxi is a lonely occupation and nothing is easier than to be ambushed.

'Anyway,' Paul continued, 'it was Pedro and his lot and he knew that I would do for him if he took any liberties with me or my car, and I told him the score, after I fought them off with the starting handle. I told them that you were just a lad learning the trade and still wet behind the ears. I told them that in any event it was my cab so they'd better lay off it.' I thought that everything had been sorted out, but then Paul added a bit that did not impress me much. 'I told them that if they wanted they could have a go at you but to leave my motor out of it.' Paul's speech put me in a quandary. On the day shift I had little cause to worry, but the start of my night shift was only two days away. Paul warned me to be careful and as I drove off the jacking lever was by my side comforting me. It was not as heavy as the starting handle but was much easier to swing about.

As I saw it, I had few options. I could go and see Pedro during daylight hours and call his bluff. I could repeat Paul's tale about me being new to the trade and unaware of the potential danger in introducing a fare who was a stranger. If it went wrong I could end up in hospital. Another idea was to visit Pedro mob-handed.

I felt I had a few friends who would be prepared to pitch in and help, but I could win a skirmish but lose the battle and the war, as they could not escort me at work. I decided that thought was required. Pedro had been rattled when attacked by a lone female. This should not be the case, so there had to be another ingredient that I had not discovered.

Then it struck me. Pedro was not necessarily afraid of the girl, but what she represented. She was the wife of arch-villain Simon and if he had damaged Simon's wife it was likely that he would finish up on boot hill. Even inside the walls of Her Majesty's Establishment Simon would still have influence and could not afford to lose face to a creep like Pedro. It was really their battle. An urgent visit to Michael was called for, and I found him pulling pints in a bar in Lothian Road. From there I went straight to the XL bar in Fountainbridge where Wally, aka 'The Wall', the equally notorious older brother of Simon, was holding court. He was dealing in the latest in a line of goods which had a tendency to fall off delivery vehicles with monotonous frequency. Suits were this week's special offer. The labels were from a reputable manufacturer and it was likely that this lot had been taken from shop or warehouse premises rather than from falling onto the road. I told the tale to Wally and he listened gravely, nodding his head from time to time and then made his announcement.

'Away about your business son and forget it ever happened. I'll get a message to Pedro.' At that time, to receive a message was to get a stripe across the face from an open razor. I genuinely did not wish that fate upon Pedro, but I did not protest either. Before I left I was offered a drink, which I declined, and then a suit. Being unsure of whether or not I would be expected to pay for it I declined that kind offer also.

I am delighted to be able to report that despite some anxious moments created by an over-active imagination, Pedro and his crew left me strictly alone thereafter. It seemed that I had new friends in low places.

12

THE PROVOST

The Provost was the most opinionated man that I ever met, and I have met a few. The annoying thing was that most of what he said made sense. He was one of those rare men who, with a few soft words, can create an argument that would have others taking sides and shouting. Minutes after entering the taxi drivers' café in the Caledonian Station he would have the place in an uproar. He was so persuasive that he always won his arguments, even when he was clearly in the wrong. Sometimes he would create an argument with a stated point of view, and by the end of it he would have completely changed tack and be arguing, without it being noticed, against the motion. He was no ignoramus and could adapt his speaking voice to suit that of his passengers. His normal accent was that of an educated man and that was why he had been christened 'the Provost'.

Approaching his fiftieth birthday, he had been driving for years. He thought that he should have had a career as a government adviser, and we all agreed. He was already working at two jobs. As a member of one of the first self-build housing schemes in Edinburgh he was under contract to labour for a certain number of hours each week, but he had also to drive his taxi full time, to earn the money to make his contribution for materials. He was a bit older than most of the others in the scheme and was unable or unwilling to take on too much of a commitment by way of mortgage. To say that he was permanently broke would be an exaggeration, but every penny he earned was spoken for.

It therefore came as a minor sensation, and the talk of the trade, when word got out that the Provost had been arrested. He had been charged with being the get-away driver in a smash-and-grab raid, and bailed to appear before the court, at an as yet unspecified future date. If convicted it would put an end to his driving career and his earnings. It would be the end of every-thing for the Provost, because without the flexibility of driving a taxi he would not be able to complete his self-build project. In short, he would face ruin.

The story as it subsequently unfolded made things look bad for the Provost. His taxi was a standard black FX3, similar to 90 per cent of the licensed cabs in Edinburgh, and it had been positively identified as the one used to raid a wholesale butcher. The location was just round the corner from the King's Theatre at Tollcross and the raid took place in the early hours of the morning. The attempt had been amateurish because entry was forced by using a sledge-hammer to the front door of the premises. No attempt had been made to disable a burglar alarm at the front of the building and it rang out loudly throughout the break-in, alerting the neighbours. The takings were presumed to be in a huge and very heavy cash register, but repeated blows from the same sledge-hammer made little impression on it. Rather than face failure the determined thieves decided to take it with them. This huge maroon monstrosity weighing nearly two hundredweights had been loaded onto the luggage section in the side of the taxi, which then drove off at high speed. High speed and an FX3 are not exactly an item, but with a loud alarm ringing and the certainty of the imminent arrival of the boys in blue, I'm sure no time was wasted.

The inevitable good neighbour, awakened by the alarm and the sound of breaking glass, had been quick-witted enough to record the number plate of the taxi. Within minutes it was being broadcast to all points by the large-booted brigade. The taxi was discovered within the hour parked outside a late-night café where the Provost was enjoying a pot of tea and a plate of petits fours. He was arrested and his taxi impounded and removed to the police garage in Heriot Row. The cash register was found halfway between the site of the robbery and the café the following morning. It had been successfully rifled and was empty. Severed screws were found jammed in the space between the running board and the luggage rack of the Provost's taxi by police forensic examiners, and paint scratches in the luggage area were a perfect match with those taken from the stolen cash register. Things could not have looked much worse. The Provost put on a brave face. He kept repeating over and over to anyone who would listen, as if it were some protective incantation: 'It wisnae me, I tell you, it just wisnae me.' When he made such protestations of innocence they were voiced in a very local dialect.

Came the day of the trial and taxi drivers occupied every seat in the public gallery of the sheriff-court and traffic jams were caused in the High Street by the accumulation of abandoned cabs. There was a palpable air of expectancy. The Provost, seated in the dock in his best suit, was wearing, for some unknown reason, a long, multi-coloured muffler, rather like Private Pike in *Dad's Army*. His hair seemed greyer than usual.

The prosecution case seemed to become stronger as the snippets of information that we had heard were confirmed in evidence. The good neighbour had only just switched off his bedside light and he was not actually asleep when the peculiar noises from the street brought him to his window. The streetlights were bright and he could clearly and unequivocally identify the registration number of the taxi being used. No, he could not identify the driver, since he had remained seated behind the wheel in deep shadow throughout the incident. The other two men he could not identify either, as they had been bent over the obviously heavy object that they were loading into the side of the taxi. They had jumped into the cab as it moved off without looking upwards in his direction.

The defence did their best. Cross-examined and accused of being 40 to 50 yards from the incident, the witness was able to confirm, having anticipated such a charge, that the distance from his window to the door of the premises had been measured and found to be 39 yards precisely. He kept a pen by his bedside since he always did the newspaper crossword before switching off his light. He flourished the pen, which had been close at hand, and the actual page of newspaper that recorded the number. The crossword had been completed. When the quality of his eyesight was called into question he stated that he only used his spectacles for close work and that his long sight was perfect. Pressed on the point he finally admitted that in fairness an 'S' on a registration plate could be confused with a '5' and an 'E' taken for an 'F'. It was possible, but not probable, that he could be mistaken. The expert witnesses for the police proved, beyond any doubt, reasonable or otherwise, that the broken screws fitted exactly the broken parts still attached to the cash register, that the paint was of an uncommon type, and equally certainly it was an exact match. They stated on oath that the broken screws and paint samples had been retrieved from the Provost's cab.

When arrested and charged the Provost had replied, 'It wisnae me.' That was his full statement. In the dock, when called upon to explain away the damning facts, he skated on very thin ice. At that time anything a policeman said in a court of law was believed absolutely.

'Ye ken, my Lord,' he began, looking at the judge over his glasses. 'I'm in a difficult position. If the polis say they found the screws in my taxi then they must hae found them there and that's a fact. But there's always bits and pieces of screws getting dropped in a taxi garage and I wisnae there when the polis found them.' The judge then asked him for a possible explanation as to how his car, which he had parked in front of the café, could have been used in a robbery, as it clearly had been, and yet be outside the café when the police arrived. Again peering over his glasses and looking the judge straight in the eye, he began:

'Ye ken, yer Honour, I'm a grandfaither – probably like yoursel' – and never in ma born days have I had a puzzle like this yin tae solve. Never heard o' the likes o' it afore. I'll tell ye what Ah think must hae happened. There's nae locks on a taxi, did ye ken that, yer Honour? Nae locks on a taxi. What Ah think has happened is that somebody has stole ma taxi while I was in there havin' ma tea, and when they've finished wi' it they've put it back – the impident buggers!'

It was an impressive example of salesmanship at its finest. Just why no one for the prosecution drew attention to the fact that, although there are no locks on the doors of a taxi, there is still the matter of the ignition key to control its use was unclear. There was no evidence of hot wiring or interference of any kind with the ignition. Perhaps the judge was impressed by the Provost's obvious sincerity and his reluctance to accuse the police of any underhand actions. In his lengthy summing-up the sheriff directed the jury that they would be required to accept that the Provost's taxi had been used to carry out the robbery. He described the Provost's explanation as innovative, and even imaginative, but stressed that this was one of those cases where they had to weigh up probability. He was a man of previously good character, but that was only one of the things to be taken into consideration. The question was an eminently fair one: did they believe his explanation? To us experts in the public gallery it seemed only a matter of time before the judge donned the black cap. It was patently obvious that he for one did not believe a word that the Provost had said. In any event, the twelve good men and true, after deliberating for just over an hour, returned the doubtful but convenient verdict of 'not proven': a verdict peculiar to Scotland.

The Provost was freed to cheers from the public gallery and a look of astonishment from the sheriff. Those who raised the subject and quizzed him following the hearing, hoping to discover the truth, were assured by the Provost that 'it wisnae me!' Something about the way he said it, and the triumphant twinkle in his eye, spoiled the effect and raised doubts. His triumph was short-lived. Unfortunately he never lived to enjoy dwelling in the house he worked so hard to build.

He died tragically young, of cancer, within two years of his appearance in court.

13

THE MILLIONAIRES' SHIP

My apprenticeship was now over, and I started up on my own with my new second-hand Austin FX3 diesel taxi, registration number LYO350, the pride of my life. By a coincidence I was exactly £350 in debt over her. The fact that I probably owned only the front bumper bar outright was of little consequence, because I was my own man at last. To bring the figures into perspective it has to be appreciated that an average week's takings from a single-driver operation was £30, excluding tips. Increasing the take by employing another driver brought its own problems. In the main they were an idle bunch and some were not averse to running with the flag up. They alienated customers by over-active use of the 'extras' button on the meter, which did not record for the benefit of the owner but was retained by the jockey. In the quirky morality of the taxi trade it was considered fair and reasonable for an employed driver to fiddle his clients, but woe betide him if he robbed his boss. He was being watched at all times and if found guilty would have a hard time securing another berth.

All new owners like me, who had no real knowledge or experience, were invariably sold taxis that, although shiny and bright, were in reality on their last legs. Before the London firms sold them on to the provinces the very best cabs had covered well over half a million miles. Mine had been running round the Edinburgh streets for at least ten years, so a million miles could have been the true distance covered. Like George Washington's axe, only the shell and chassis were perhaps truly original, but to me, at that particular moment, there was no better cab on the road. I was to learn that maintenance is expensive and all that glisters and all that is so true. I had been broke before I bought the taxi, so nothing changed despite my confidence that it would.

Because cabbing is a cash-handling business there was a permanent temptation to dip into the takings. They were mine after all, and sweets, food, newspapers and a hundred other basic necessities drained away the profits. The 'extras' button, which I had hardly ever used, became important now that the revenue raised by it was mine. The easiest way to earn extra cash was to find work that took you beyond the limits set by the Public Carriage Office. Going out of town allowed you to negotiate the fare with your client. Two areas were of particular importance to Edinburgh cabbies. The US Base at Kirknewton was a good bit beyond the city limits as agreed by the Public Carriage Office, but the Yanks were relatively well paid and mostly bartered over their fares, so that was no problem. The other opportunity was when asked to take a fare to Queensferry. The border here was at the top of the Hawes Brae, only half a mile short of the ferry pier. Fares there were mostly Royal Navy sailors from Rosyth trying to get back to their ships. Most of the taxi drivers were ex-servicemen and were happy enough to take the odd Jolly Jack Tar right to the ferry for the recorded fare. More often than not if there were five of them they would happily divvy up the twenty-five shillings between them. This gave the driver the best part of ten bob for himself, which was more than enough to keep him solvent for a couple of days. The cab still earned the essential shilling a mile. The fares we hated were the know-alls, usually civilians, who would request a trip to the top of the Hawes Brae only. The only pleasure we got then was seeing them turn themselves out into the rain if the weather was bad.

When news of the imminent arrival of a shipload of mil-lionaires who would disembark at South Queensferry came through, we were ecstatic. The day had to start off well with a 25-shilling run to Edinburgh as a minimum. Being millionaires, they would be ideal customers and the anticipated tipping memorable. Some remembered the American aircraft carrier fiasco and decided to give it a miss. I had fond memories and laid my plans carefully. Some taxi drivers were a disgrace to the calling. Historically, cabbies had been exposed to the elements when they drove their hansom-cabs, and the habit of wearing several layers of grubby clothing was a long time in passing. There were no regulations by the police-controlled Cab Office governing personal hygiene, and some unshaven jockeys could have benefited from an extended immersion in sheep-dip. On the other hand, my car was gleaming inside and out and a new tartan travelling rug was neatly folded on the back seat. I was wearing 'the suit', my only suit, a particularly smart Prince of Wales check three-piece in a pale green instead of the more usual grey. Brown suede shoes, a dazzling white shirt and a dark green bow-tie completed the ensemble. I got some curious looks from other cabbies.

Only about a hundred Edinburgh licensed cabs had turned up and hackney operators from Queensferry and various pirates made up the numbers. As an early riser, I was cab number seven on the rank, but it did not make the long wait any easier to bear and we had no idea how many passengers would be coming ashore, or when. The ship was a big one, too big to enter any available docks, so passengers would arrive in dribs and drabs, delivered by a small motorboat. With luck the early birds like me would get two runs in at least.

Little doubt it was after having enjoyed a late shipboard breakfast that the first of the Americans came ashore, and because it was mid-morning they were in no hurry as they drifted towards the line of taxis. They were much taken with the Forth Bridge and photographed it constantly. It became clear at once that they, being millionaires, were a bit fussy. By tradition clients took the first cab from the head of the rank and as the cars moved forward they took pot-luck. Not this lot, they didn't. Our transatlantic visitors decided to rewrite the rules. They walked up and down the rank inspecting the taxis and drivers before making up their minds whom to select. It has to be admitted that the more disreputable the driver the louder his protest at this flagrant breach of the 'rules'. We felt like a cross between wallflowers at a dance and second-rate whores in a Port Said brothel, although I should quickly point out that, although I had spent two years in Egypt, I had no experience of brothels in Port Said, or anywhere else for that matter.

As in most cases, youth has its value and a handsome couple quickly snapped me up. He was distinguished-looking with silver hair, and had plucked me out of the line to the distress of the drivers ahead of me in the queue. He was, it turned out, a successful surgeon used to getting his own way. He was also an enthusiastic bird watcher. She was slim and elegant, and when we reached the top of the Hawes Brae they had me stop while they photographed the ship framed by the bridge. I was able to answer all their questions about the bridge, which was a bit of a fluke because I had recently been reading about its construction. He nodded in agreement at my replies and it came to light that they had been issued with a booklet on the bridge and my answers confirmed the facts stated within it. My stock rose several points when he realised that I was a person that he could trust.

He quizzed me about the robin-redbreasts that might be found in Scotland and I was stumped. It was his passion and I knew next to nothing about them and had only really noticed them on Christmas cards, but that was about to change. He told me that the American strain was much larger than the British counterpart, as it would be, and that he was determined to see and photograph a local one. It was agreed that we would keep our eyes open in the hope of spotting one of those elusive birds. I thought for a minute that Edinburgh Zoo would be the place to try but had a rethink and kept my mouth shut.

He and his wife had a bit of a chat and they decided that they would like to hire me for the day. A fee of ten pounds was agreed and their first request was simple to fulfil. Could I recommend a good hotel for lunch? This was a surprise, because I had been convinced that they would only recently have left the breakfast table, though popular fiction had it that Americans ate all the time. On second thoughts, they obviously ate sparingly because they were both slim and trim. I had heard good reports about the Norton House Hotel, although I had never dined there, because people like me didn't. Since we could quite easily drive past it on the road to Edinburgh my advice was accepted without questions. Having been brought up to believe that Americans were the most democratic of people on earth I was looking forward to lunching with them, and finding out more about them, and about America for that matter. I saw nothing incongruous at the prospect of an impoverished but very well dressed taxi driver sitting down to dine with a mega-rich and renowned surgeon.

When we had completed the trail up the mile-long drive and crunched to a stop outside the imposing entrance I could tell by their reaction that I had chosen well, as this was clearly their kind of place. As I slid from my seat to open the door for them, as they obviously expected I would, I felt rather than heard something tearing, and a chilly breeze suddenly assaulted my nether regions. The sharp end of a seat spring had poked through the hide seat cover and torn the backside out of my trousers. One minute I was looking forward to being invited to dine in style and the next I was in utter despair. The Findlay clan is made of stern stuff and the show had to go on. My right arm rigid by my side holding the flapping trouser seat tightly in place with my right hand, I skulked round the rear of the cab and opened the nearside door for them. Half-hiding behind the opened door, I made sure that they remained in front of me at all times. My guests had noticed nothing but they were not as democratic as I had imagined. They were snobs, and snobs don't dine with their servants. 'Let me see,' he said, glancing at his wristwatch. 'Shall we say an hour for lunch? Pick us up at 1.15. I'm sure you can get something to eat in the servants' quarters.' I smiled my thanks and murmured my acquiescence and would have done a good hand-rubbing imitation of Uriah Heap, but I only had one free hand. I departed for the back door with as much dignity as one can muster while shuffling backwards holding one's torn trouser-bottom in place.

The hotel staff were magnificent and the housekeeper, shaking her head in disbelief, examined my trousers.

'I'll do my best but I can't promise much. These look beyond repair to me.' Quite naturally she held them up for the cooks, waiters and waitresses and all passers-by to view. She disappeared from the kitchen tut-tutting away to herself and I was left standing in the middle of the kitchens in my rather short shirt-tails. I still had my jacket and waistcoat, my bow tie and my socks and shoes. My legs were bare from my socks to the top of my rather attractive thighs. It was like the last act of a farce just before the curtain falls. There would be no curtain-fall to hide my embarrassment. A chair was offered and there I sat, making the best of a bad job while tucking into a wonderful steak and chips garnished with a baked onion and a whole cooked tomato. As I munched my way through this excellent repast the waiting staff passed and repassed my table giving me nods of encouragement. The housekeeper's staff, having been given sketchy details of the strange trouserless man in the kitchens, made feeble excuses and came through to see for themselves. My pudding was tinned fruit and Carnation milk. A glass of beer was served with my steak and I had cheese and coffee served with a Hine brandy to end the meal. It was all the more enjoyable because it was all being charged to my undemocratic American cousins. When my trousers were returned the housekeeper was full of apologies.

'They are completely beyond repair I'm afraid but I've done the best I can.' For the first time I got a good look at the damage. The pointed piece of the spring had held them fast as I rose from my seat and the resulting tear was 'L'-shaped, with each edge being ten inches long. I thanked her and everyone else in sight profusely and carefully donned my trousers before I returned to the cab. A pair of pliers, after a struggle, bent the offending metal to a safer shape, but the stretching of doing that simple job had caused the repair to gape open in places. When my passengers exited from the hotel I was in position half behind the door, holding it open for them. When they were inside I slid all the way round to the driver's door and eased myself very carefully down onto the seat.

A tour of the city was next, and although the weather was fresh rather than cold, my clients were disinclined to disembark. We drove round Arthur's Seat and then up the Calton Hill to enjoy the views to the north. We then drove up to the Castle Esplanade and down the Mound. From time to time they did get out to take photographs and those most democratic of people always waited for me to open and close the doors for them. I was happy to do this, but always made sure that only my left hand did any work, while my right was kept by my side holding on to my dignity. My clients were only ever exposed to the left-hand side of my body. I slipped up by not taking them to either the zoo at Corstorphine or the National Museum in Chambers Street, where information on the red-breasted robin would have been easy to find. To satisfy his need for a sighting my client had me drive them out into the country, but Mrs Hubbard's cupboard was right out of robins. We passed the time to everyone's satisfaction; they asked questions about nearly everything they saw, with me spinning convincing yarns to satisfy their curiosity. Back in the city I had them near to tears about the fate of Greyfriars Bobby and they, who by now realised that a flying visit would not suffice, changed their plans.

On impulse they decided that they would stay overnight, as millionaires can, and knowing my clients by now I took them to the rather swish Caledonian Hotel. The pound–dollar rate of exchange was calculated very much in my favour and I was paid off with a bundle of single dollar bills which included a more than generous tip, all doled out into my left hand. His last words to me proved that, although a snob to my eyes, his heart was in the right place.

'Son,' he informed me gravely. 'I don't want to embarrass you or anything like that, but I just couldn't help noticing your arm and how conscious you are of it.' At this point he produced a card from his top pocket and handed it to me. 'As you know, I'm a surgeon, and although I say it myself I'm a damned good one. If ever you find yourself over Stateside be sure to look me up, because I'm sure I could get some mobility into that arm of yours.'

Man is never so vulnerable as when his backside is exposed to view unintentionally. Having slipped home to change into the other 50 per cent of my wardrobe, I was ready to face the world again. Not only was I feeling better, being in my blazer and slacks, but my arm had miraculously healed and I needed to strike before the iron cooled and find myself more wealthy Americans as passengers before their ship sailed. It is easy to spot American tourists in Edinburgh. Their top coats are often very light cream or even white, while their skin has a healthy tan. Their hats are colourful, and as often as not above the ubiquitous camera they sport something in tartan round their necks. I had marked out my next fare. It was around eight o'clock in the evening and I was certain that my prospective passengers would most likely be heading back to Queensferry to enjoy dinner on the millionaires' liner.

A 25-shilling fare, plus tip, was all the incentive I needed to give them priority over any other persons who might be seeking cabs at that particular moment. I therefore ignored two different raised arms in Princes Street to oblige our overseas cousins. The American gentleman was, true to form, wearing a tartan scarf round his neck. When he and his wife settled in the back of the taxi he unwound it to reveal a dark blue tie emblazoned with a pattern of square and compasses. His blazer pocket had the same design embroidered into it and he wore a lapel button of a similar insignia. On his left hand he wore a large gold ring that again had the square and compasses built on it in a rather ostentatious design. My alert brain immediately told me that he was a Freemason. The subject that he wanted to discuss with me was Masonry in Scotland.

'Could you direct me to a Masonic lodge, brother? Any one will do just fine.' This was his first question. I was not a mason but we taxi drivers have an encyclopaedic knowledge of our city and I had a ready answer.

'They advertise the meeting in the local newspaper, but usually at least a day ahead, so without yesterday's *Evening News* I think you'll be out of luck. Besides, although they advertise the times that they meet, and the streets where the lodges are, they don't give details. I also think you'd be a bit late for tonight, because from what I've read they seem to kick off at seven o'clock or seven-thirty at the latest.'

'Gee, that's a pity, my lodge is affiliated to the Scottish Grand Lodge and I thought that there would be no difficulty in visiting one over here.'

Again I put him right, although we had not moved an inch. 'I'm not a Mason myself although my father was, but he's dead now so he can't help; if we can find a street where a meeting is being held we could probably track one down by following the men who wear black ties and carry wee cases. But as I've told you, I think that you'd be too late for a meeting tonight; they will all have started by now.'

'Gee, brother, that's a real shame. I had my heart set on making a visit and seeing the difference in our workings.' He had lost me by now and I had my heart set on a run to Queensferry. Then a thought struck me.

'I don't think women can attend lodges, so what will your wife find to do if she can't get in?'

'Gee, I forgot about that.' He pondered for a moment and I put my foot in it as far as a run to Queensferry was concerned.

'The Grand Lodge of Scotland has its head office in George Street.' I knew this because it had been one of the questions asked by the Cab Office police inspector when he had questioned me on my knowledge of the city. 'But of course they will not be open until tomorrow morning.'

'That settles it, brother. We would probably be late for dinner on the ship, so we'll stay overnight, just take us to a good hotel.'

On the journey, which was not very long, I quizzed him on Masonry. I told him that in Scotland it was a secret society that seemed to me to be very hush-hush. Was it the same in America? I naturally did not mention that no one who met him could be in any doubt as to his membership of a so-called secret society.

'In the States we are proud to be members and to us it's not a secret society, but more of a society with secrets. It's even in the language. You've heard of guys getting the third degree when the police beat them up? To us it's just a club for men. It lets us have a night off from our wives.' His wife was not best pleased and spoke for the first time.

'Oh, Elmer.' She sighed aloud, making the two words sound like a whole sentence. He just had to be called Elmer. He was probably used to the words of reproach as a severe telling-off. We had arrived at the North British Hotel and he produced a bulging wallet to pay me the paltry fare. 'Gee, brother. I've only got big denomination bills; a twenty is the smallest I've got, I don't suppose you've got change?' He supposed correctly but came up with a solution. 'I tell you what, brother: you pick us up in the morning at ten o'clock and take us to the Grand Lodge, and we'll see where we go from there. Is that OK?' The man was a Mason, so of course it was OK. He was kind enough to give me his all-American name – Elmer K. Kawolsky.

I don't suppose I need to tell readers that when I called the following morning at ten o'clock on the dot at the North British Hotel it was to discover that my American cousins, surprise, surprise, were not waiting for me. In fact, when I enquired at the reception deck for them, there was no record of any Kowalsky having registered. I hate to be beaten over matters financial and so I made it my business to visit the Grand Lodge of Scotland without delay. It was a very imposing building, and there were lots of things there that would have impressed Elmer no end, but whether he visited and saw them I will never know. The custodian was adamant when I told him my tale. 'We've had nae Americans here the day, are you sure that you're at the right place? If they was masons they wouldnae let you doon. Their word is their bond, ye ken.' He then added a few words that reminded me that the sectarian divide was as wide as ever in Scotland, 'If they owe you money there's the Knights o' Saint Columba roon here someplace, so you should try there.'

14

HIGHLAND DONALD

I was sitting on the taxi rank on the High Rigg at Tollcross, indulging in my favourite pastime of people-watching, when I saw a head. It was higher than those surrounding it, and whereas they progressed in a level flow, this one went up and down, up and down, like a yo-yo. It was a very strange movement and the owner of the head, as I was to discover, was equally strange. He was much taller than most and wore a student's scarf wound tightly round his neck. The scarf was so long that it reached his knees fore and aft. When he was all of fifty yards away some sixth sense told me that he was heading for my cab. It also told me that we would be in conversation very soon. If my sixth sense had been a seventh one I might have driven off and never met him, but I continued to sit there waiting. That is how I met Highland Donald.

Before he arrived I had made up my mind about him. He was, in my opinion, a country boy, but that was the easy bit. Farmers, and others who stride across fields, have that quirky walk. The other thing that I divined correctly was that he had a problem and that it would inevitably become mine. I was right on both counts. Most fares jump confidently into the cab, state the desired destination, and that's it. Donald stopped at the driver's window. He was another Hugh, like my love rival for the sexciting dental nurse, Fiona, and they spoke in the same manner and dialect. They might in fact come from opposite ends of the same island. He only wanted directions, the bane of a taxi driver's existence.

'Would you be knowing the whereabouts of the International Bar please? I haff to meet someone there.' It was an easy one to answer.

'Take a left for two hundred yards, if that, and it's on your right.'

'Would you take me there do you t'ink?' I was amused that an educated person would speak in this quaint manner. For the first time in my life I turned down a fare. It was probably my sixth sense struggling to become a seventh.

'It's not worth it since it's only a few yards and you can't miss it, honestly.' To come off the front of the rank for such a short run is uneconomic. It was 1.30 on a nice sunny Wednesday afternoon, half-day closing for most of the town, and sometimes after a suitable period for refreshment a shopkeeper would indulge himself with a taxi home to the suburbs.

The High Riggs rank was unique. The first cab sat in the middle of Tollcross and my position, first reserve as it were, was sited by a cab company service telephone, so I had two chances of a fare. It was treated as a separate rank and a driver was entitled to pick up without asking the prospective fare to go to the cab on the Cross. I did not want to lose this popular position for a mere two-bob ride, but Donald was insistent.

'When I meet my friend we will be going on to somewhere; I don't know where yet, but we will be going on, so you will get a good fare out of it.' He then added, slyly, 'and a good tip too, I'm t'inking.' He had me hooked and we were off. I have always been a sucker for those three little words. No, not 'I love you' but 'here's a tip'. Two minutes later we were parked in Tarvit Street opposite the side entrance to the International Bar. The clientele were far from being an international in-crowd. It was the haunt of American servicemen and their camp-followers. A much more discreet crowd than used the Berkeley in Lothian Road, but a clique nonetheless. It now became apparent that the young Highland gentleman of the serious mien had further requests to make.

'Would you be a good fellow and go into the bar and tell my friend that I am here? I am not used to public houses and such places.' Taxi drivers get used to dealing with all kinds of people and his request seemed quite reasonable. All the same, I sensed that this man, who was younger than I was but called me a 'good fellow', was a bit of an oddball, so I said no.

'Look mate, there's the door, go in and collect your pal and I'll wait here.' He looked as if he was about to burst into tears.

'Oh dear,' he sniffed. 'That wass not my plan at all. I haff never been in such a place hass that in all my life and my friend will be waiting for me and everyt'ing.' He was becoming quite agitated and a worried expression had settled on his face. I would not forget in a hurry my run in with Pedro the Pirate the last time I acted on behalf of a fare, but I found myself feeling sorry for him despite this. He was clean and tidy, with 'student' written all over him. Quite good-looking and well-built, so a pub should hold no terrors for him, especially at lunchtime. I still had a funny feeling about this character.

'Look,' I said, realising that I was in a win-win situation. 'I drive a cab for a living and a penny a minute waiting time is not going to make me rich. Pay a deposit to the fare up front and I'll go in and get your pal. I am not going to risk you nipping off while I'm inside.' He was shocked at the suggestion.

'But I would neffer dream of doing such a thing. I am a man of honour. My word hiss my bond,' he protested. I nearly quoted the old hackneyed line. 'In God we trust, all others cash', but I was not out to amuse. I was out to make my living so I gave him an ultimatum.

'I do believe you, I really do, but now,' I held out my hand, 'fare up front if you want me to run about for you. Otherwise pay me off and I'll go, because I've wasted enough time.' My face must have revealed my frustration.

'Do not take on so,' he muttered. 'Here hiss a pound. Hiss that enough?' I was happy now. He then gave me my instructions. His pal turned out to be a girl called Moira who was evidently an habitué of the International. She could also be found in all the other bars that catered for our American cousins. All I had to do was to let her know that her friend Donald was waiting in a cab outside and she would come at the double. Although it was a midweek afternoon the joint was jumping, as the saying goes. I had to force my way through a scrum before I could get to the bar and catch the barman's eye. In response to my whispered request he nodded to the far corner where a group of girls were being entertained by some uniformed Yanks. The jukebox was right next to their seating and I had to shout at three different girls before one, claiming that she was Moira, acknowledged me. These girls, it seemed, often used different names on different occasions for reasons best known to themselves. We went to a quieter corner.

'There's a young student in my cab asking for you if you're Moira. He wants you to come out to see him and he told me he had come to pick you up.' A pained expression crossed her pretty face. Her bone structure was excellent but acne had ravaged her cheeks in adolescence. Apart from that blemish she would have been classified as truly beautiful. The damage had no doubt resulted from her own negligence. As a teenager she had probably covered her acne with cheap make-up and rouge instead of medicinal balms, and the legacy would last her lifetime. Above her prominent cheekbones two large almond-shaped hazel-coloured eyes shone brightly. Clear, true and innocent. Her figure was trim and her clothing immaculate and fresh. Only her voice let her down, badly, as it identified her area of origin in this, the snobbiest city in the universe. She had clear intentions of becoming a GI bride and in the States her accent would be considered 'cute' and typically Scaddish. In Edinburgh it clearly identified her as being from the wrong side of the tracks. This was a real pity, because with a little time and effort this Eliza Doolittle could have passed for a duchess.

'He's not a guy called Donald, is he?' Moira was anxious to know but did not wait for my answer. 'He's a right pain in the ass and I can't get rid of him. Tell him I'm not here.'

'Tell him yourself. He's just outside in the cab. I'll see that he behaves himself.' As usual I couldn't keep my nose out of other people's business.

'OK.' agreed Moira. 'But you be there all the time, right?' I gave the necessary assurances.

Now, it is fairly well known that I am not the heroic type, but show me a damsel in distress, and I'll be there like a shot, particularly if she has big round hazel eyes and a cute figure. If she's fat and fifty, I admit I can't be relied upon, but I knew that I could handle this Donald if he became stroppy. Moira told her friends that she would be back in a few minutes and I escorted her across the street to the taxi. As she climbed in I slipped behind the wheel. I was amazed to hear, as the partition between us slid shut, Moira's voice exclaiming, 'Hello again, darling. You've no idea how much I've missed you . . .' With that the partition was closed. I could hear no more but I watched the proceedings through my tiny safety mirrors, since Moira's safety was paramount. For a pain in the ass Donald was doing OK. They kissed and cuddled and there was some earnest conversation, most of it when they took it in turns to whisper in each other's ears. Neither of them used Traffic Warden Hugh's blowing technique so I was unable to see it road-tested. Body language gives a lot away and the more he pleaded the more coy she became. He promised, she agreed. At last the partition was opened again.

'Right, driver,' ordered Donald, with a ring of confidence in his tone. 'We're going shopping and Moira will give you directions.' This she did, and they were very specific.

'Take us to Richard Shops on Princes Street, but go by George Street and then wait in Frederick Street. Have you got that, driver?' Ten minutes earlier I had been her Young Lochinvar and now I was reduced to driver. The Princes Street shops were all closed, as I knew quite well, and to be told to go the long way round was music to my ears. It was none of my business if they decided to include me out of their plans. The partition slammed shut and the two lovebirds sat together as close as Siamese twins. If this was how Moira treated pains in the ass it was high time I became one. When we parked up in Frederick Street the delightful Moira skipped off down the street, turning from time to time to blow kisses to a very chuffed Donald lodged in the back of the cab. With the partition open Donald and I made small talk.

'She hiss a wonderful girl hiss she not?' sighed Donald rhetorically. 'A wonderful girl. It hiss such a pity that she hiss addicted to the drink, you know. Oh yes, it hiss a real pity. But I am working on her and her love for me will be stronger than her love for the drink I am t'inking.' The only thing that I was thinking was that Donald was not thinking, or if he was thinking he was not thinking straight. I had met Moira for the first time only half an hour before and she may well have been an addict, but not for drink. My guess was that her addiction was to easy money. From the moment she had given me the elaborate instructions to visit the shops I had smelt a scam, because I'm quick like that, but it was none of my business. If Donald was the mark, well, he was getting the hugs and kisses. The only possible answer to his comments was to agree with him.

'She really hiss a lovely girl, Donald.' I was about to add that he was a lucky lad too, but that was still to be proved. As we waited, he expanded on the development of his love affair with Moira and, probably in an attempt to make me feel jealous, confessed just how naughty they were planning to be.

'She hiss off to get some exciting underwear to make our first night together very special. She hiss getting stockings and everyt'ing. She hiss really in love with me to do it because we are not married or anyt'ing, not even engaged!'

I did my best to look aghast, surprised and happy for him, yet envious all at the same time; which was difficult. Donald was beside himself with suppressed excitement. The meter was ticking towards the two-pound mark when Donald decided that he had better lead a search party to find out what was keeping Moira.

'Not until you pay me, Donald. Another pound, if you please.' He was not going to do a runner on me. 'Another pound will keep things right.' But Donald was full of surprises.

'But I haff no money left. I gave my wallet to Moira so that she would not be short when she was choosing the exciting underwear and everyt'ing.' The gullible Donald's protests fell on deaf ears and in the end a very subdued Donald agreed to meet me on Friday night to settle his dues. On the strength of this understanding I dropped him off at Surgeons' Hall.

It was then that I had a flash if inspiration. It was a great idea: in future I would start to carry only passengers where I could hope to receive payment.

15

TEMPUS FUGIT

In the film *The Bridge over the River Kwai*, the Japanese went to a great deal of trouble and exercised fiendish ingenuity to construct a suitably cruel punishment chamber for Alec Guinness. A far simpler, but equally harsh, design could have been achieved, if they had simply forced him to drive an Austin FX3 diesel taxicab. He would have been frozen stiff at nights and been done to a turn during the day. Whoever designed the taxi had certainly never driven one in earnest. It was cold, draughty and damp in winter. When hot weather struck, as it sometimes did even in Edinburgh, it transformed itself into an oven and you roasted. There was no happy medium.

It was the height of Edinburgh's typical summer season, two or three days of sweltering hot weather, with not the slightest breeze to bring relief. I had been sitting in my cab, my shirt sticking to my back, longing for even a puff of wind to remind me that this heat could not last forever. I was on a rank I rarely used, one at Roseburn, not a great pick-up point. A mark seven Jaguar purred to a stop on the opposite side of the road and I could not fail to notice the driver. She was a ravishing brassy blonde, a real gangster's moll type, as seen in the movies. She was looking cool and elegant in a low-cut dress. Her companion in the passenger seat dismounted and waddled across to where I was sitting. He was as noticeable as she was, but for a different reason. He was wearing a heavy Crombie coat, tightly buttoned, which apart from being ridiculous in the oppressive heat made him look top heavy.

His foxy face was friendly enough but he looked anxiously up and down the road before he spoke. He was a Scouse with a Liverpool accent thick enough to cut with a knife. It took me a moment or two to tune into it and understand him.

'Wanna watch boss? Wanna watch?' He spoke out of the side of his mouth and his eye winked furiously as he talked. 'Good gear, straight up, all the cabbies know Scouse, famous I am, you can do yourself a right favour. Lookee 'ere. Any kind you like.' He could certainly talk, but as to his claim to fame I for one had never heard of him and never heard his name in the taxi canteen. As he said his piece he pulled up the sleeves of his coat in turn to reveal watches strapped to his arms from wrist to elbow. The sight clued me in to what he was talking about.

'What lorry did these fall off then?' My remark brought a pained expression to his face.

'I told you boss, it's all straight gear.' I needed a watch as much as I needed an excavation in the cranium, but there again, it's hard to resist a bargain. 'Look,' insisted the bold Scouse as he opened his coat. Draped in row upon row, each watch minus a strap and held in place by a safety pin threaded through the strap barrel, he had at least fifty different dials on display. When he opened the other side of his coat the display was doubled in size. There were too many to take in all at one glance. Each side of his suit jacket was opened in turn and more stock was revealed. A third layer was pinned to his waistcoat.

How he could breathe with so many layers of metal draped over him, all retaining heat, was a wonder.

'The best are round my legs,' boasted Scouse. Bending with difficulty, he pulled up a trouser leg to reveal another display.

'How hot are they?' was my next sally.

'Hot!' Scouse recoiled in mock horror. 'Hot! Me sell a hot watch? Never. They may be a bit warm temperature-wise seeing as what the weather's like, but hot, never.' His patter was good but unconvincing. Everything about the whole set-up shouted 'crook'. My morals were seriously brought into question. Taxi drivers are honest upright citizens and it would be stupid to risk a reputation for a few quids' worth of watch. But there again . . .

'Have you got a gent's really slim wristwatch?' Someone had told me that a sure sign of quality in a watch was how slim it was, and I believed it.

'Here you are boss.' Scouse had dived into a pocket and produced a nice-looking watch with a gold-coloured finish. 'How about that, boss?' He certainly knew his stock. It was exactly what I was after. Ten minutes ago I had had no thought in my head about a new watch and now I was really fancying this one if the price was right. With hindsight, I should have forgotten about the watch and registered the question as an intellectual title. 'The price is right' has a certain ring to it! I had the watch in my hand and was waiting for Scouse to quote me a price. The auction started in earnest.

'Fifteen quid,' Scouse opened the bidding. I offered a pound. A pained expression was my reward, but no bad feeling developed.

'At ten pounds I'm robbing meself, honest, boss. I only let you taxi drivers have a cheap one each because you bring me tons of business.' The haggle continued. The watch had a slightly metallic tick but it seemed all right to me. The dial was really attractive. I was up to two pounds and ten shillings, with Scouse stuck at six pounds when his blonde piece tooted the horn of the Jaguar in what can only be described as an urgent fashion.

'Quick,' exclaimed Scouse. 'The bizzies are coming. Do you want it? Four quid for a quick sale.' I shoved it back in his hand. If the police were around I had no desire to be shopping for stolen goods. I did not know if the watch was any good or not, and I had come across the real experts during my time in Port Said. Scouse waddled back to the Jaguar and they roared off. I waited apprehensively, but no policemen, police vans or police cars passed, so it must have been a false alarm.

Over the next two weeks every cabbie in town was sporting a new watch. Some of the more enterprising were selling them on to their passengers. The Princes Street watch shops must have noticed a sudden downturn in trade. Every hook, crook and comic singer was flashing a brand new timepiece. The big black Jaguar ghosted about all over the place. Barmaids, bus drivers, bookies' runners and anyone and everyone had a new ticker. It was crazy. They acted like newly engaged girls, but it was wrists that were flashed instead of third fingers. They were desperate to show off their newly acquired trophies that had been such a bargain. Five years of normal trade in watches must have been achieved in as many weeks, all of it garnered by the enterprising Scouse, who seemed to lead a charmed life, but was sure to be riding for a fall. Curiously enough, I was there when it happened, and I was one of the few who had failed to fall for his blandishments.

Saturday night found me as usual at the 'cleaners' – our shorthand for Powderhall Greyhound Racing Stadium. Taxi drivers were allowed in free of charge after the third or fourth race, so it was a popular venue during a normally quiet time for trade. Arriving late allowed us to study the trends of the evening's racing and a 'taxi drivers' system' had been devised that never lost. Whichever trap was the first to win twice would invariably win a third time during the eight-race programme. Clearly the system has to be tweaked to take into consideration the odds on the dogs running out of that particular numbered trap. Losses were doubled up and winning nights frequent. I had just invested my two bob forecast on the tote when I spotted Scouse.

He was watching for anyone who had a big win from either the tote or the bookies. As they were counting their winnings Scouse would sidle up to them and the coat-opening and sleeve-raising would commence. As often as not a transaction would take place. A little later two security men moved in on Scouse from opposite directions and he was grabbed and frog-marched away. I was a bit sorry for him, but his dealing had become more and more flagrant, so it must have been only a matter of time before he fell. I had a feeling that lots of plods would be wearing new and free watches before long.

Later on Scouse reappeared. He was still operating, but much more discreetly than before. The two security men were adjusting their new watches to match the correct time as recorded on the stadium clock. I had had no idea that such bribery and corruption were so rife. No wonder he had been able to run his sales operation so freely all over town; I had a sneaky regard for the guy. In fact, I was kicking myself for not buying a watch that first day when I had the opportunity. He was certainly slick and bold, and he worked hard at his trade.

A few days later I bumped into Paul, my friend and mentor, and told him the story. Like every other greedy person looking for something for nothing, or at least a bargain, I had conned myself. Scouse's stock was entirely legitimate and he carried receipts to prove it. He bought imported and rubbishy watches very cheaply in Liverpool. The blonde was Mrs Scouse and the Jaguar and the tooting of the horn when Scouse gave a pre-arranged signal were all window-dressing to get you to bite. Paul's final admonition has stayed with me. He was adamant that if a thing seems too good to be true, it usually is.

Another lesson learned and another milestone passed on the road to becoming a proper, and worldly-wise, taxi driver.

16

BERT'S KIDOLOGY

That we are all 'Jock Tamson's bairns' was one of Bert's favourite expressions and for a policeman it was an ideal philosophy. He hated the injustices in life that he found while going about his lawful duties and did his best to rectify such matters where and when he could. He was a first-class copper, being one of the old school and more than a bit resistant to the political correctness that was even then working its way into the service. Policing was in his blood and if he had a fault it was in his attitude to neds, teds and everyday criminals, because he loathed them. He was particularly hard on those who were foolish enough to break into a pensioner's flat where they raided their coin-operated gas or electricity supply meters and were then unfortunate enough to get caught. He had a frightening attitude towards any villain who raised his hands to girls, wives, mothers, grannies or old ladies. When they fell into Bert's capable hands they were inclined to mend their ways. It may be my imagination, but it strikes me that we had a much more effective police force in those days. A certain height, potential weight, given time, and width of shoulders were considered essential ingredients in recruits. When a policeman walked the beat he had to be a man who was respected. The populace trusted a local policeman and he picked up every bit of information, ranging from who had done what to whom to the names of those planning to do what and when. He locked up grandfathers, fathers and sons from the same families during his career and knew just when and where to find them. The system worked.

Bert was highly intelligent and had real musical talent. His time in Malaya with a Highland line regiment had taught him drumming and the rudiments of piping, and he was good enough to be a member of the Edinburgh City Police Pipe Band when they were awarded the World Championship. On this occasion the mischievous twinkle had left his eye when we spoke. His summer had been spent travelling round Europe with the band, but it was back to beat work for the winter months. Petty jealousy made some senior people resentful of the night shifts that had been missed while the band drank strange beers in foreign parts. Those same envious bosses were now hell-bent on making sure that the band members played catch-up.

'It's the night shifts, Dougie. I'm out of practice and it's getting me down. Those all-expenses-paid trips abroad representing Edinburgh; well somebody had to do it, but it's back to auld claes and parritch now and I don't like it.' I commiserated with his lot, despite being quite jealous myself. The tales from the European tour would make anyone envious. His scale inspector, who was tone deaf, insisted that he and the others had so much to learn that they had to attend lectures during the day and work night shifts as well.

'You won't believe what the latest course is about. It's called "Psychology and the Criminal Mind". Did you ever hear of anything as daft?' Bert was horrified by what he had learned. 'There's no baddies now. It's the fault of the environment that they were brought up in, and being deprived as kids it's not really their fault when they go wrong.' He gave a wolfish grin. 'We have to try to understand them. It's psycho-ology, not kido-ology mind, but psycho-ology, that's the order of the day.' Bert broke the words into five syllables with such deadpan expression that I was unsure whether or not he was serious.

'What's the big idea then, Bert?' I was genuinely interested because, driving a cab, you had to be a bit of an amateur psychologist all the time. 'Will it help you to catch more villains?'

'What?' Bert recoiled in mock horror. 'Catch them and take them before the courts so that they can get a slap on the wrist? You unfeeling taxi-person you, why you no listen?' I was suitably chastened. 'It's not their fault. I already told you that. We've to understand their point of view. What's more natural if you've not got a car or if you can't afford one, than to take or borrow one that happens to belong to someone else? Notice I said borrow? They do not steal, they just borrow. Unless they intend to permanently deprive the owner of the vehicle then it's just a misdemeanour. When we've cracked the psycho-ology caper we will have what is called the psycho-ological advantage over the neds.' Bert beamed broadly at his neat encapsulation – a full day's course into a couple of sentences. Despite Bert's efforts I was not yet clear on how it was supposed to be put into practice.

'Well, Dougie, it's like this. I've been doing the psycho-ology thing for ages without realising it. Take last night, it's a typical example, it's just come to me.' Bert stroked his chin and looked thoughtful for a moment. 'Fancy me being an expert without realising it. This is a good illustration of how it works. Anyway, here's what happened. We'd been told to keep a lookout for a particular stolen car, an Armstrong Siddeley, a big beauty it was, and I spotted it and flagged the driver down and he stops the car, good as gold.'

Bert went through a pantomime as he spoke. Looking through an imaginary telescope he scanned the horizon, looked down as if scanning a list of numbers on a non-existent piece of paper before holding up his hand in a very regulation manner to stop this figment of his vivid imagination. It was quite a performance and I felt that I had been there and seen it for myself. 'As I step forward I clock the tax disc and the registration number. I open the door.' He interrupted the narrative to ask me if I had seen the door on an Armstrong Siddeley. I had, and confirmed that it was a great heavy door that opens outward from the hinges in the middle of the car.

Bert went on. 'There's a young well-dressed chap behind the wheel and he looks as cool as a cucumber. I says, "Good evening, sir, lovely evening for a drive", and I smile like a crocodile, showing plenty of teeth, you know what I mean? "Sorry to stop you, sir, but I have to enquire, is this your own vehicle?" His neck must have been made of brass and we could have weighed it in at Bernard's yard for a week's wages. "No, Officer," he says. "It's actually my father's car, but he's out of town at the moment and he lets me drive it naturally enough." "So you'll know the registration number then?" He trots it out.' Bert was now looking perplexed. I butted in.

'If it was his dad's car he was hardly likely to press charges against his own son was he?'

'You know, Dougie, for a minute he had me going. He must have designed that course that I was on because he was beginning to get the psycho-ological advantage over me. But I KNEW it was stolen. Anyway, I had to play by the rules, so I prattles on. Could he tell when the road tax was due for renewal? I had him there. "Oh," he says. "My father sees to all that sort of thing." So I try a dodge of my own. "Would you mind stepping out of the motor, sir, please?"' Bert went back on stage and into his Sir Walter Raleigh routine, spreading both hands out in a sweeping gesture towards an empty space.

'What did you do then, Bert?' Bert was a wily character and the punchline had to be near. When it was delivered it was a real punchline.

'Dougie, as he stepped out of the motor I gave him a skelp across his lug. You never saw anyone go down faster in your life. That's when I recognised my mistake in doubting our lecturer, who was dead right all along.'

'What do you mean?' I demanded. 'Right all along? That wasn't what they taught you on the course, surely?'

'Well,' Bert admitted. 'Not the actual methodo-ology perhaps, but a triumph for the new police training methods. I never thought I'd see the day that I'd admit that they were right.'

'Come on, Bert. I still can't see the connection.' I was really trying, but could not link the theory to the action.

'Simple, Dougie,' explained Bert, his eyes twinkling. 'I had got the psycho-ological advantage at last and I was on top of the situation. He was that busy worrying about when I would hit him again that he coughed on the spot: not only to taking the Armstrong Siddeley but to half a dozen other offences forbye.'

17

TOMMY

Tommy was drunk and I had never seen him in that condition before. He was, to quote his own words, 'fu' as a wulk'. So full was he that he was holding his bottom lip out as if afraid that he would spill some of the expensive fluid responsible for his sorry condition. He was crabbing along with the purposeful air of one who feels that one false step would lead to downfall and ruin, and the chances of regaining an upright posture nil. I watched him approach from my position on the rank at Surgeon's Hall. He was wearing his usual uniform of dungaree jacket and wellies, but his flat cap, usually worn down over his eyes, was well back on his head and exposed a forehead of pale white skin that was usually concealed from daylight and protected from the weather.

This was a new Tommy. Normally he kept his eyes downcast and avoided catching anyone's eye, especially when in conversation, which was a rare event. Tommy mostly walked backwards, over years of practice he had found this the best way to progress. It could be that he was the inspiration for the Goons' famous Christmas song about walking backwards for Christmas. In his working hours he usually walked backwards because he was a scaffy, and that was how the streets were kept in pristine condition. The long witches' broom-type scaffys' brushes were rowed rather than pushed. Although the work that they did was vital, the city council took advantage of this band of dedicated men. In lieu of a pay rise they were promoted to the rank of street orderly. Tommy was extremely proud of his status and never tired of telling the few people that he spoke to that he worked for the 'corpy', before adding the rider, 'tempry-like'. Poor Tommy had been a temporary employee for a dozen years or more, and his dearest wish was to become 'pernament-like'. Tommy and his band of brothers kept the Edinburgh streets as clean as any city in the world. To aid his endeavours he was provided with transport. A two-wheeled double-binned barrow that was, like the witches'-broom brushes, unique to the city. Edinburgh in the 1950s had a surprising number of horses using its streets, and consequently the plentiful horse droppings were a prime target for Tommy. This skilled operative, walking backwards and sculling away like an Olympic oarsman in a dry-land regatta, could clear a street hundreds of yards long in minutes. The muscle power required must have been considerable, and Tommy had not an ounce of fat on his frame. Being classified as a temporary employee meant that he did not have a regular place of work. He stood in for those who were sick, on leave, or had died, probably from exposure to the germs that were part and parcel of their lives.

Tommy was not all that popular with his workmates because when he stood in for them the streets concerned seemed to sparkle. There was also jealousy over his barrow. Tommy washed and polished his twin-tub special with the same care and attention as that lavished by a motorist on his first car. It was adorned with the discarded favours of any football team that visited Easter Road or Tynecastle. There was never any fear of his pride and joy being up-ended by visiting hooligans because their team colours would be represented somewhere on his barrow. He was a very shy and retiring man who was not overly endowed with grey matter, a fact that would colour any remark that he made, but he was making something of his life. He worked hard and never missed a shift, and was apparently without a single vice. At least, that was what I had believed until I saw him in this clearly inebriated state. In fact, I would have laid a sizeable wager that Tommy would be teetotal. That extrovert tendencies lurked within was evident from his colourful barrow, but in every other respect he seemed as shy as a violet. Clearly drink made him a bit more sociable.

Arriving at last at the cab he grabbed the door handle for support and peered at me, obviously having trouble in focusing, and enquired, 'Hit ish you innit?' He paused for breath and narrowed his eyes, the better to see. The effort of speaking and looking at the same time seemed too much for him. 'Yeah, hit ish you right enough. Just the man.' Tommy lapsed into silence for a moment or two and swayed unsteadily. 'Mr Finnally, Ah wunner if you can help me.' The title of 'Mr' meant nothing to me. Tommy called everyone he was obliged to address 'Mister'. With Tommy real respect kicked in at 'Sir' and rose as high as 'Your Honour'. Having confirmed that it was indeed me he was addressing he sighed heavily and lapsed into silence. I asked what I could do to help. 'Hows about takin' me hame, Mr Finnally? I'm drunk, an' that's a true fact.' It was an offer that I could not refuse, as the saying goes; but before I allowed him on board I read him the riot act as to the cost should he be sick in my taxi. He appeared contrite and mumbled an address before slumping down on the back seat in a comatose state. His usually weatherbeaten face was deathly white and a few beads of sweat adorned his forehead. It crossed my mind to do a Burke and Hare and drop him off at my friend the embalmer, Mr Abbot, but I understood the demand for fresh corpses had dropped off somewhat of late.

Home was a dank, dark tenement building off the top end of Leith Street, long since mercifully razed, and when I arrived I anticipated problems. Drunks are always a problem for cabbies. However, the few minutes he had spent in the lad of nod had worked wonders on Tommy. It may have been fear at being near home, but whatever it was, he was much revived. His mental state seemed normal, but his legs were not in such good shape.

'If you just sit me doon here for a meenit or so Ah'll be fine.'

'Doon here' was the first step of the tenement entrance. Tommy grasped my hand, not, as I first thought, to pull himself upright, but to congratulate me.

'Thanks, Mr Finnally, you're a true pal an' that's a true fact. Look at me an' the state Ah'm in. Better no go intae the hoose just yet or the wife'll batter me. Ah'm no actin' much like a dad.' Life is full of surprises and this was a double whammy. For no justifiable reason I had never imagined Tommy would be married. He was certainly old enough, being late thirties or early forties, but his shyness? He was clearly not all that shy if he had a youngster, but Tommy in the role of husband and father took a bit of believing. From his seat on the cold steps Tommy continued to praise me to the heavens and described me as the best pal a man could have. In vain I pointed out that driving people home was part and parcel of my business, but he kept on and on.

'Naw, Mr Finnally, you dinnae unnerstan', you hardly ken me an' you've drove me hame an' every'hing.' It was about now that I realised that one small part of our business contract was not going to be fulfilled. I was clearly not going to be paid. 'Ah've nae dough, Ah'm skint Mr Finnally, spent it on the booze. But Ah'll pay you the morrow. Don't you worry. Ah'll be in aw day, don't forget now, number twel'.'

I was fed up with Tommy and his ramblings and had some money to make. I fired up the old diesel and was off.

It had been a hard day and night because trade was patchy, and I just kept on working to keep the finance company happy. It was mid-morning on a Sunday, because on single manning you were forced to work the best hours, and often they were when the more experienced cabbies had, sensibly, gone home to bed. It was getting close to the point when I would be forced to call it a day when, quite by chance, I found myself driving up Leith Street. I had mentally written off Tommy's fare, but the idea of a few coppers more for no extra effort grabbed me, and I turned off and drove to his door. It would also be interesting to see Tommy playing happy families.

The tenement smelt damp and there was a creepy chill in the darkened interior when the front door closed behind me. Living in a dump like this would be enough to break anyone's spirit and I felt sure that most of the residents, being at the very bottom of life's heap, must have settled for their lot and written off any hope of moving up or bettering their lives. No wonder that Tommy had got himself drunk. I groped my way through the gloom, tripping over broken flagstones and up to the second landing where the air seemed fresher. 'Fresher' is a relative term because there were no windows to admit daylight, no gas light-ing that I could see – although it may have been simply that all the mantles were broken – and communal toilets were located along one wall.

The nameplate on the door was the only bright spot I had seen since entering the building and it gleamed like a welcoming beacon in the gloom. The legend 'T. Souness' was embossed in black lettering, and under the name the number twelve. There was no bell-pull or button to push, so I rapped on the door panel and waited. And waited some more. Within I could hear the creak of floorboards, first to the right and then to the left, and I convinced myself that the door was not going to be opened at all. After some more shuffling, the creaking stopped, the door was thrown open and light and heat flooded out onto the landing. Tommy stood framed in the doorway dressed in exactly the same rig as he had been wearing before, but now his cap was back to regulation level.

'It's yersel', Mr Finnally, it's yersel'.' His greeting was warm and sincere. 'Come away in.' He then added sotto voce, 'Ah'm in a better state the day than Ah wiz the ither day an' that's a true fact.' As he stepped back to make room for me I crossed the threshold and stopped in open-mouthed wonder at room number one of the two-apartment dwelling known as a 'room and kitchen'. There was nowhere for me to go. I had never seen anything like it in my life. It was crammed with furniture of every description. Bright, highly polished, cheap, old-fashioned, poor-quality tat. I did a double-take, not quite believing my eyes.

Tommy was watching my reactions closely. The wall that could be seen, that is, the bits that did not have furniture resting against them, was festooned with pictures and plaques. One mirror had a remarkably bad illustration of a lady in a crinoline dress fashioned from strips of coloured paper and it had been very amateurishly executed. A second mirror, even larger, depicted an underwater scene, complete with treasure chest and sunken galleon. The plaques were plaster of Paris and in various sizes. One represented a World War I zeppelin and another a London street fair. Finding a spare square inch of wallpaper would be a problem.

The pieces of furniture ranged from an unmatched pair of tallboy chests of drawers to several Formica-finished cabinets in a variety of colours. One sported a frosted glass front and another clear glass, with a third in a solid wood veneer-type finish. There was a Welsh dresser, several tables, bookcases sans books, and every inch of shelf-space filled with china and brass ornaments. A roll-top desk that Ebenezer Scrooge would have been happy to call his own took pride of place and backed onto the settee of a three-piece suite.

Whatnots and what-have-yous were squeezed onto any spare floor area, even under tables. A giant television set, the biggest I had ever seen, rested on a table facing the Welsh dresser. Between them there was just enough room for a single upright kitchen chair. The viewer must have felt part of the action. Nine, ten, twelve and in an exceptional case a fourteen-inch screen were known to me, but this piece of apparatus must have been twenty-one inches at the very least. I presumed that either Tommy or his spouse must be very short-sighted.

The room contained so much furniture that it was impossible to walk across it in a straight line. Everything on the floor formed a maze, so that doubling back and finding blind alleys was the order of the day. Hampton Court had nothing on this lot. Two items that stick in my mind were a lamp in the form of a fully rigged sailing ship. The light that emanated from the port-holes was neither use nor ornament as far as a reading light was concerned, but the red and green of port and starboard and a flashing white masthead lamp made an interesting conversation piece. The other was a globe of the world, with the British Empire painted scarlet. There was an abundance of light in the flat, since any spare level surface carried a lamp of some sort or another. Where a standard lamp could find no space on the floor it was stood on a table where it just touched the ceiling. The entire ensemble must have cost a fortune in electricity and could have given the Blackpool illuminations a fair run for their money. Despite the clutter the room was spotless, with every surface reflecting and enhancing the brightness of the wattage. Tommy was delighted with my reaction.

'Look under the tables, Mr Finnally,' he urged. 'There's mair stuff there.' And there was. Cylinder vacuum cleaners, a spin-dryer, a gramophone, a couple of electric fires of interesting vintage and a twin keyboard typewriter (one for capital and one for lower-case letters). A wide range of aids to twentieth-century living were all deposited there, as well as some very interesting-looking boxes and parcels. Tommy's heart was gladdened by my startled reaction to this Aladdin's cave of treasures.

'No bad fur a workin' chap, eh, Mr Finnally!' His chest swelled as he spoke. I was so astonished that the truth blurted out.

'I've never seen anything like it in my life, Tommy; some of that stuff will be worth a mint some day.' I now understood the position. In his work as a scaffy he must come across loads of rubbish that people had discarded. That would explain it. He then offered me a cup of tea. It had been, as I have already mentioned, a long and trying day plus a night and a day, so I accepted gratefully. As he brewed up at a cooker parked directly in front of the only window in the room he explained that his wife and son were out on an errand at that time but they would return any moment. He was most anxious that I should meet his wife and his son and heir, wee Tommy.

Finding somewhere to sit proved to be difficult but Tommy, with superior local knowledge, led me unerringly through the labyrinth to a seat between two tall objects. From this vantage point I could hear him but only see his reflection through a triple arrangement of mirrors. As we walked, Indian file, to this spot the floor creaked ominously and I had visions of falling to a premature death impaled on shards of old wardrobe. The downward rush would be terrifying as we fell through two floors to end with a sickening thud in the sub, sub basement. It could be years before our bodies were found. My musings were interrupted by the arrival of a watery cup of tea, a lot of it in the saucer, and with tea leaves floating on both surfaces.

'Ah've put plenty sugar in, you'll like that,' Tommy stated confidently. I had last taken sugar in my tea years before, at the start of the war, but I agreed with him as it seemed less bother. At this point the door opened and Mrs Tommy and issue appeared. Shyness must have run in the family, because when junior caught sight of me he gave a squeak and disappeared underground to his normal, if his pasty face was anything to go by, troglodyte habitat. I saw him no more but did detect stealthy movements in various parts of the room from time to time. I judged that he was around two years old. Mrs Souness was clearly painfully bashful too, and she coloured a bright pink and hung her head when Tommy tried to introduce us to each other. Instead of stopping to talk she slid past me to take up a position by the sink and busied herself in polishing the taps. Once or twice I thought I saw her glancing in my direction, but it was hard to tell, since her eyes faced in opposite directions and the glance was liable to have been deflected by two or more mirrors before arriving into view.

'Ah wiz just tellin' Mr Finnally aboot oor stroke o' luck, hen.' This announcement caused Mrs Tommy to start, and she whispered something to him, and blushed crimson this time as she turned her head away and started to polish a kettle. The cryptic message, double Dutch to me, caused Tommy to reassure her. 'It's aw right, hen, Mr Finnally is my pal and he'll no tell nobody.'

By now I wanted to hear the story and slid my unwanted cup of tea out of sight. I pressed him for details of their stroke of luck. Had he won a small fortune on the football pools?

'Naw, naw, Mr Finnally, a'body asks me that 'cause they want to ken how Ah got ma furnitire an' that.' Tommy perched himself on the end of a table to increase his comfort.

'Let me see,' he began. 'It wiz two, naw Ah tell a lie, it wiz three year ago an' Ah wiz walking doon the Stockeree ken, an' Ah must hae been lookin' a bit doon in the mooth 'cause Ah hears a voice an' it's saying tae me: "Hello, Tommy, you're looking awfy sad, what's up?" It wiz yon Mr Binnie, him wi' the furnitire emporium, ken.' At this point the reader should be made aware that Binnie of Binnie's Furniture Emporium was a crook much admired by the cognoscenti in Edinburgh. He specialised in house clearances, robbing widows of their mite, and selling on antiques for a fast buck while stocking his three shops knocked into one with any rubbish he had left. He was an ideal man to buy from if a subsequent fire insurance claim was being arranged.

'An' Ah says tae him, "Ah'm sad, Mr Binnie," an' he says tae me. "You look as if the sky has fell on yer heid, Tommy." So Ah says tae him, "The sky *has* fell on ma heid, Mr Binnie." So anyway he says tae me, "What's the matter?" So Ah tells him. Ah've got a lassie intae bother and Ah've got a hoose off the corpy but Ah've nae furnitire and nae readies tae buy none. "Tommy," he says. "Tommy, your troubles is over." An' Ah can tell you Mr Finnally, ma troubles wiz over an' that's a true fact. Mr Binnie took care o' every'hing'. I'nt that right, Lizzie?' Lizzie squeaked in a fair imitation of Junior's utterance a few moments before. During the tale she had remained silent apart from a gasp when their marital secret was revealed. But now she was nodding vig-orously in support of Tommy as she rubbed away at an upright surface. She actually echoed his last two words, 'worries over'. With practice she would probably break into speech in a month or two. Perhaps that's why wee Tommy put in his appearance. She perhaps did not care to speak to a stranger, even to say no.

My heart bled for Tommy. Binnie's advertised that your penny was worth a pound at his store while the reverse was true in practice. Red flag sales kept him going nicely and he worked on the principle that there really was a mug born every minute. At Binnies', hire purchase was really higher purchase. Every piece of consumer protection legislation has a loophole, and Binnie always not only found it, but also enlarged it. Old goods were sold as shop-soiled and shop-soiled as new. He was a very sharp businessman, and Messrs Dodson and Fogg would have been putty in his hands. This was Tommy's benefactor. As he stressed, 'Mr Binnie supplied every'hing. Carpets, rugs, ornaments, pots an' pans, cups and plates and knives and forks an' every'hing.' Tommy marvelled at the generosity of Mr Binnie.

'How much did it all cost, Tommy?' I was anxious to know. Tommy brushed aside my question. Binnie would have been impressed by his star customer.

'He did us proud, did Mr Binnie. Ah says tae him, "Ah'm no kiddin', Mr Binnie, Ah've nae money fur a deposit nor nuthin'." Ye ken what Mr Binnie says? He says. "Deposits is for mugs, Tommy, leave it tae me." What dae ye think o' that?' I thought that I would like to know how much it had all cost. I pressed him on the subject. His eyes narrowed and his face clouded in an effort to recall details. Binnie was a past master at vague con-tracts. Actuarial adjustments were made to ensure that clients were never released from debt. 'Mr Binnie said that Ah wiznae tae worry aboot any o' that stuff, he wid see tae it aw. He kent Ah worked for the corpy but Ah wiz fly, Ah never telt him Ah wiz only temp'ry.' I had Tommy on the run at last and pressed him on how much he repaid each week.

'It depends, Mr Finnally, if Ah hiv' a good week Ah pays a bit mair and if it's a flat week a bit less. Ah've explained that tae ye. Mr Binnie sees tae aw that. He has the figures at 'is fingertips.' As his new pal, I felt duty-bound to protest.

'Tommy, look at the place, you've got far too much furniture, and you don't need it all.' In reply I got three pitying looks. One from Tommy and one from each of Lizzie's eyes.

'Mr Binnie says that soon naebody will be able tae get stuff like this and if we get it noo we'll be ready when we get a bigger hoose. He's no mug is Mr Binnie.' Realising that I was fighting a lost cause I pointedly looked at my watch and said it was time I was on my way.

'You canny go yet, Mr Finnally, you havnae seen the rest o' the hoose, you've no' seen the bedroom.' I was led to the second chamber of the tiny apartment. Lizzie was becoming quite bold and, duster in hand, followed us through. The room was a replica of room number one but white goods were much more in evidence. It takes away the boudoir feel when a rusty refrigerator, indoor clothes airer and washing-machine dominate the romping area. Then there was Junior's cot. The item that really caught my eye was an ancient upright piano fitted with drooping candlesticks that semaphored a distress call. Instead of white and black keys it had cream, tan, brown and some that were completely missing. It was of German manufacture and should have been snapped up for the then current craze of smashing up pianofortes and shoving the pieces through a six-inch-wide hole in a wall. On second thoughts, a single team of a dozen men would have no chance of lifting it clear of the floor. I looked pointedly at the piano, and then at Mr and Mrs Souness. A conspiratorial smile flitted across their features. This was clearly a well-rehearsed party piece.

'I didn't know you played the piano, Tommy.' I was certain that Tommy would have difficulty in working out how to lift the lid, but played along.

'Naw, no me, Ah don't play it.'

'Mrs Souness?' I didn't believe it but I had to ask. 'Do you tickle the ivories?' Tommy answered for her. She had the ghost of a smile on her face and Tommy's face was set in a slight grimace in what I took to be an effort not to smile.

'Naw, Lizzie disnae play it neither.' There was a definite smile on its way now and they were on the brink of unleashing some terrific joke. I pressed on regardless.

'Let me get this straight. You have a piano, right. You don't play it and your wife doesn't play it, so why do you have it?'

'It was Mr Binnie's idea, Mr Finnally; it's fur the wee fella, the bairn.' The Sounesses were fighting back their laughter as he said this and I was completely mystified. I wanted to get a dig in at the artful Mr Binnie.

'Tommy,' I said slowly and pedantically. 'Be logical, the kid is only two. It will be years before he could be considered for lessons and you've had the piano for two years already.' Tommy and Lizzie broke down at last and burst into paroxysms of uncontrolled laughter at my failure to spot the obvious. Shaking his head from side to side Tommy looked at me in sympathetic amazement, incredulous that someone like me could be so obtuse.

'You've still no got it, Mr Finnally, you've still no worked it oot.' He laughed aloud at my discomfort. 'An' it's that obvious and everybody kens it.' Tears of mirth were now rolling down their cheeks as they held each other upright, laughing at my stupidity. 'It's just like Mr Binnie says,' cried Tommy, wiping tears from his eyes. His wife meanwhile was hugging herself in sheer delight. '*A'body kens it's good fur a bairn tae grow up in a musical envir'nment!*'

It was only when I was back in the cab and driving off that I remembered that Tommy had again failed to pay his outstanding fare but, thinking of how much he would owe the Binnie emporium for the rest of his life, I decided to write it off.

18

MACTRAVEL

In 1952, when I was doing my bit defending the Canal Zone of Egypt on behalf of king and country, my Liverpool lovely wrote to tell me that she had booked a holiday in Spain and was travelling by air! Such a thing had never been heard of before. She and a bevy of Littlewood's Pools' employees were part of only the second package tour to the Iberian sun at an all-inclusive price of £25. This was expensive in those days, and it was exciting stuff since the old converted wartime Dakota aircraft were not pressurised and as a result had to take the long way round to avoid mountain peaks. The aircraft was obliged even to refuel en route. It was well worth the effort when they discovered that a tumblerful of 103 Brandy cost only an old penny, equal to virtually nothing in today's currency, and everything else was equally inexpensive. On the down-side, there was little to do except swim in the sea and lie in the sun, or so she assured me by pen pal letter. It was clear to me that the idea would never catch on.

Only a few years later I came across a man who knew better. He was the sole proprietor and founder of MacTravel in Castle Street, Edinburgh. He was into package holidays in a big way by then and he was the early bird who was catching worms by the bucketful. His business was expanding at a tremendous rate as he tried to corner this lucrative market for himself. I had signed up with City Cabs and MacTravel gave the group a lot of business. Quite by chance, this was to be my first call to the MacTravel offices. Drivers were always keen to take his work because in addition to the decent tip that was invariably added to the fare, the journey could be anything from a station pick-up to a jaunt in the country. He was constantly showing off to men in grey suits the latest batch of hotels that he had gained exclusive rights to use. He was a great one for carrying out snap inspections on hotels and supervising the conversions to en suite facilities, an essential if he were to satisfy his growing American trade. Such facilities were scarcer than hen's teeth in the Scotland of that era.

Mr MacTravel had a very short fuse and an explosive temper, and was used to getting his own way. His account was valued, and in accordance with City Cab policy I only dropped the flag 100 yards from his office so that the minimum fare would still be on display should he choose to check it. Before I could make it known that I had arrived, a small group trotted down the steps and across the wide pavement to the cab. I knew at once that it was the great man himself because his bearing radiated confidence. He was young to be so successful, being mid-40s at my guess, and no one could be in any doubt as to who he was, or that he was the boss. His immaculately tailored suit shouted Savile Row, and the shine of his shoes glinting in the mid-morning sunshine would have gladdened the heart of a drill sergeant from the Brigade of Guards. His snow-white shirt dazzled and the subdued patterned silk tie was in perfect harmony with his desired image. He looked what he was, a very successful businessman, and a man who has everything. A minion carried his topcoat, briefcase and travelling case, had a note pad in one hand and an uncapped pen in the other. Despite his burden he was making notes on the run. An elegant woman, similarly suited and equally well groomed, was in attendance. She was the second Mrs MacTravel, his former secretary, the one he'd married for her looks and because the first Mrs MacTravel had found out about their affair. She fussed over her husband too much, perhaps betraying a degree of insecurity, as they approached the taxi.

'Don't worry, darling,' she reassured him. 'Robert is perfectly capable of standing in for you for a few days. He does exactly what you tell him to do, so he's more than capable of standing in for you. You're always in a rush. You must relax more.'

'Four days is a lifetime,' growled her husband. 'I've half a dozen important deals in the air at present and if I lose one of them I could lose them all. There's a lot of money at stake.' They were seated in the cab by this time. The MacTravels were in the back seat and Robert perched on one of the tip-up seats facing them. 'Robert, if anyone tries to pull a fast one or if you have the slightest doubt about anything, do nothing at all. Consult Mrs MacTravel about anything that troubles you. She knows how my mind works and she will guide you.' Robert was too old to be the son, even from the first marriage, so he was probably a personal assistant. The cut of his suit was good but not in the same class as that of his boss. Everything indicated that he was in an inferior position in the business.

'Don't you worry, sir; Mrs MacTravel will approve any moves I make while you are away.' Robert spoke with confidence-building assurance. The list of things to attend to grew longer.

'Those Gleneagles bookings, don't forget to confirm. And the Canadian crowd, tell them I'm sorry to let them down by not being here personally to greet them, and I want you to convince them that my trip is a matter of life or death. Sit on the coach prices until I get back because I'm sure we can get a better deal. Remember to talk to Simpson . . .' The flood of words was non-stop until we reached the station. During the journey Mrs MacTravel had said very little; she could hardly get a word in edgeways. She gently brushed imaginary hairs from the shoulders of her husband's suit and chided him to relax. She was very beautiful, but she might as well not have been there because he ignored her completely. Young Robert 'Yes sir'd' and 'No sir'd' in the subservient way that was obviously required of him. When we arrived at the station the omniscient MacTravel turned his attention to me.

'Right, driver,' he barked. 'Wait here until they see me off. When they come back, drop Mrs MacTravel at Forsyth's in Princes Street and take my manager back to the office.' When I left the RAF I was determined that I would never again take orders from anyone and would never address a person as 'sir' unless my respect for them had been earned. Now that MacTravel was paying the piper and I was chasing a wage I had to dance to his tune. I obediently responded, 'Yes, sir, I'll see to that.' And I gave him a bashful smile that perhaps impressed him as to my humbleness because he instructed me to add 15 per cent to the bill. No words like 'thank you' or 'please' were in his lexicon. As I smiled properly in gratitude I hoped that he couldn't read my mind. With that the duo departed for the platform and Robert, having rushed ahead despite being laden down with the luggage to buy platform tickets for him and Mrs MacT, looked exhausted. I watched as she ushered her husband into the nearest first-class carriage. As he leaned out of the window to give her a farewell embrace he took time out to issue further orders to the hapless Robert. His deputy was still scribbling away as the train drew slowly out along the platform. In response to her husband's wave Mrs MacTravel dabbed her eyes with a tiny hankie. Once the train was out of sight Robert ushered Mrs MacTravel back to the taxi and sat beside her on the back seat. He suddenly began to imitate his boss by issuing orders.

'Change of plan, driver,' he announced. 'The MacTravel Mansion on the Lanark Road as fast as you can.' At that he reached forward and slid shut the glass partition between us. As the old taxi growled up the incline of the station approach, Robert pounced on an extremely willing Mrs MacTravel, who was clearly an accomplice in his dastardly design. Unknown to the combatants, my secret little safety mirrors were working overtime and they provided me with an exciting if limited grandstand view of the proceedings. They kissed and cuddled for the entire journey. Mrs MacTravel was a gorgeously attractive woman and Robert, just as long as the affair remained a secret, one very lucky young man. All this before noon in Presbyterian Edinburgh! Too soon, we crunched up the gravel drive to the imposing pile that had become the new seat of the MacTravel Clan. The pair unglued and with as much dignity as she could muster under the circumstances a pink-cheeked Mrs MacT, realising perhaps how indiscreet they had been, fled from the cab. With the front door-key held aloft, perhaps as a talisman to ward off evil thoughts from a taxi driver's head, she disappeared into the matrimonial home. Robert, a much cooler customer, was left to sort things out. Handing me a 10-shilling note he successfully guaranteed my silence and he reminded me to claim my 15 per cent tip when submitting the bill to the MacTravel accounts department. His parting comment convinced me that he would go far in any business.

'My boss,' he lamented breathlessly as he adjusted his tie, 'expects me to do everything for him while he's away.'

19

THE OFFER

The newly opened late night café in Montrose Terrace must be offering good value, I thought to myself, because at least thirty taxis were parked outside it. Why I was late coming on duty that particular Friday night, I can't remember, but I do know that I wanted something to eat before facing the hurly-burly of a busy night's cabbing. My luck was out, but Pete Chalmers, a driver I hardly knew, was clearly enjoying more than his fair share. He was standing on the edge of the wide pavement chatting to two absolutely gorgeous girls. As girls do, they were almost identical in dress, and could have been twins. Both had long blonde hair that was not obviously suicidal and dyed by their own hands, but if not natural, the change had been wrought by an expert and expensive hairdresser. They each wore tailored black suits, black patent leather handbags and matching shoes, tan stockings, crisp white blouses, a single gold brooch on the jacket lapel and a gold necklace. As I say, I hardly noticed them as I made my way to the door of the diner. It was then that I heard Pete's voice.

'Hi, Doug,' he called. 'Just the man. Can you do me a favour?' Instinctively I knew that he wanted something, because I can be quick-witted at times. He was greeting me as if we were firm friends, and I was happy to become one, if I was going to be introduced to this pair of top-drawer dolly birds. They seemed to hang on his every word as they gazed at him adoringly. I wondered if he had won the football pools' top prize. What on earth had possessed him to bring them to a place like this? The Caledonian Hotel would have been much more suitable.

Pete had a reputation for unreliability, in a trade that is unreliable by its very nature, so, although I was wary, I responded in kind and smiled back at him.

'Sure, Pete, how can I help?' Both girls glanced in my direction and I was the subject of inspection and appraisal. They independently nodded approval and gave me the benefit of their super-white smiles. An unworthy thought jumped into my mind and I banished it instantly. The favour obviously involved the girls, so whatever it was, I was willing. There is no point in being an eternal optimist if you allow the odd set-back to get you down. If he was after a loan of cash he was out of luck, as I had not yet turned a wheel, and was virtually stony broke. 'Would you give one of the girls a lift home?' he queried. 'I'd take them both but they live in different directions.' I would be prepared to do this kind of favour all day long, but as usual with Pete there was a sting in the tail. 'They're friends of mine, and a bit short of the readies, but you'll get your fare, I can guarantee it.' It was no big deal and would simply mean that I would start work without a meal to sustain me. 'Lynn lives off the Queensferry Road so it's quite handy really,' Pete went on glibly. I was hardly listening because I was being pressurised by dazzling smiles from the two beauties. The one that became my fare was Lynn, who was the elder of the two by a couple of years, and strangely enough the one I would have chosen if choice had been a factor.

It was just after eleven on a fine Festival night and during this period it was as if the clocks had been put back. Everything happened later than on a normal night. Business would not pick up until after midnight. Queensferry Road was like a rat-run for taxi customers. They would dance all night or whatever, and then set off to walk home to the various schemes to the north-west of the city. When they got fed up walking, or if it started to rain, they would hail a cab. Once on that side of town it was unlikely that I would stray far from it all night.

I tried not to be too eager as Lynn and I walked back to my taxi. Some men can attract women without effort, while others, like me, find it hard going. I could do the chat bit with very little effort, and make them laugh, but that was about it. Lynn was good company. She spoke well and smiled a lot, and even laughed at my feeble jokes. Pete had guaranteed me my fare so she had no need to be too grateful. I thought that she was delicious and I am sure that she was shrewd enough to know that she had made an instant conquest without the slightest effort. Beauty is in the eye of the beholder, and I have had many truly beautiful women in my taxi, but many of them I would cross a street to avoid. They can be vain and a pain, but Lynn, as lovely as any of them, seemed to be completely genuine and down to earth. She was not wearing a wedding ring, and this surprised me. Either she was extremely fussy, or was on a second time around journey, seeking security. Before we drove off I turned in my seat, ostensibly to get detailed directions, but in actuality to give her a really critical assessment. She was far from perfect. Her eyes were too large and too blue. Compared with her friend Pauline her figure was fuller, her breasts a little rounder and her legs longer. She was a ten.

Lynn spoke, 'It's really good of you to go to all this trouble for me, Muirhouse is such a long way.' Muirhouse? Pete had told me Queensferry Road. 'I'll be able to pay you back on Tuesday, Wednesday at the latest.' The back end of the taxi was growling away, warning that a new phosphor bronze crown and pinion would be required very soon, and telling me I needed to raise cash without delay. I had also received a billet-doux from the hire-purchase company reminding me that our agreement was that I would make repayments regularly.

Despite this I heard myself declare that the payment of the fare should be the least of her worries, and that I could wait as long as it took. I glanced at my secret mirrors to monitor her reaction and was rewarded with a breathtaking glimpse of stocking top, as she crossed those shapely legs. Her skirt rode up enough to leave an inch or two of creamy white flesh on permanent display. I wondered if I should let her know that I was watching her, but before I could do this, she made a comment about nothing in particular. It was then I noticed it, a slight slurring of her words; she was a little tipsy and I hadn't realised it before. Perhaps it was the alcohol percolating through her system? The address in Muirhouse was a block of council-owned flats in a rough area. Things did not quite add up; there was something of a mystery about this well-spoken woman. When we drew up Lynn made no move to alight. She was in a mood for talking and I had no need to quiz her. I was sitting comfortably sideways in my seat with my elbow resting on the division. Lynn relaxed on the back seat. The sky was light and the moon very bright, and in the half-light of the taxi she looked good enough to eat.

'I bet you're wondering why I'm living in a dump like this?' Lynn could add mind-reading to her many attributes. The story unfolded and I discovered that she had lived in England until recently, and life had been fine until the marriage had turned sour. Being good Roman Catholics, divorce was out of the question, as was contraception, according to her husband, who held the purse strings. Three daughters were enough for Lynn but husband did not subscribe to birth control. He wanted a son and heir and was prepared to keep going until his ambition was achieved. Her sexual embargo led to rows, and rows inevitably to separation, when Lynn and her brood fled north. She joined her sister in Scotland where, within a few weeks, a council flat was made available. Hubby, resident in England, refused to send a single penny to her, caring nothing for the welfare of his brood. Advocates advocated doing nothing. The Church wrung its hands in impotence after declaring that Lynn's problems were all self-inflicted, announcing that she had a clear Christian duty to return to her husband and breed. She was in a catch-22. I indicated my support by nodding in all the right places as I listened.

'I suppose that I should be grateful to the council for this flat and everything, but it's such a contrast with how we used to live. We've been here for a year now, and instead of things getting better, they're getting worse. Then I met this man.' It was inevitable that with a woman as attractive as Lynn one would always have to *cherchez l'homme*. Nature abhors a vacuum and without trying Lynn would create flames round which replacement husbands would gather en masse. I was not surprised to discover that there was a man in her life. I would have thought a regiment was more likely. Lynn's voice became plaintive. 'He's a really nice man but he's made up his mind to go to Australia and he wants to take me and the girls so that we can all make a fresh start. I can't get a divorce, and without it we can't go. This man is determined to go to Australia, with or without us, so we've broken up.' She looked really depressed as she said this.

'This guy of yours must be crazy, but he'll be back.' I assured her.

'No,' sighed Lynn. 'He won't wait. It's over.' She sniffed a little as she opened her handbag and produced a combined cigarette case and lighter. She clicked it open and reached out her arm to make me an offer.

'Cigarette?' she enquired. 'Damn and blast it, I've only one left.' As a confirmed non-smoker this was no problem for me. I was enjoying listening to Lynn's voice, but the role of father confessor did not sit well on my shoulders. Suddenly Lynn brightened. 'So tonight, I said to myself, the hell with it. Went on the town with my sister and spent my last bean. God! I must be mad. My last penny in the world – gone.' She was not a lot older than I was, probably six or seven years, but her life experiences were out of my league. My troubles seemed minor when I considered hers.

'What am I going to do?' she groaned, and the momentary brightness departed, and gloom descended. 'I've no cigarettes for the morning, and I doubt if there's enough milk for the kids' cornflakes. Some mother I've turned out to be.' With a self-deprecating grimace she prattled on. 'Left the kids in on their own all night and went out and spent what little money I had left on trying to cheer myself up. Not even a shilling for the gas or electric meter. What will I do if it runs out?' Breaking off from her discourse she raised her head and looked me straight in the eye with those big, big baby blues.

A flash of inspiration seemed to flash across her face. She shared her idea with me. 'Doug, how would you like to sleep with me?' I couldn't believe my ears and nearly fell off the seat. 'You can if you give me two pounds.' My throat was dry and my palms damp. She took my silence for a refusal. 'Thirty bob then; surely that's not too much to ask? I'm really desperate for some cash so I'll make sure you enjoy it.' I wanted to accept this wonderful offer but my over-active imagination was working overtime again. The old 'what-if' syndrome. My chaste lifestyle meant that I had no need to carry protection and Lynn, being a devout Catholic, was probably in the same boat. In the RAF we had been shown films of unfortunates ravaged by the untreated conditions brought about by unwise romances. There were other thoughts too. Taxi drivers had been known to be lured to dark places, with the promise of a delivery of forbidden fruits, only to be rolled and robbed. Even if it was all above board, I would want to stay all night, and I'd miss the best night of the week's trade. I was also extremely short of ready cash and I doubted if I had as much as a pound about me. I could perhaps get rolled, but I couldn't get robbed. There were no holes in walls at that time which spewed out money on demand. Now, being older, and I hope much wiser, my answer would be very different. Then, I tried to have my cake and to eat it as well.

'I'll tell you what I'll do, Lynn,' I stammered, and I should have come clean and admitted that I was flat broke, but that did not occur to me. I fumbled in my pocket and gave her about ten shillings in coins. 'That's the meters taken care of. Tonight I'll buy some cigarettes from a machine and put them through your letterbox for the morning, and when I get up to town I'll buy a couple of cartons of milk from the new machine in Queensferry Street and leave them on your step for the morning. Trust me,

I'll see you right. How will that do?' adding as an excuse, 'I really do have to work.' I was so stupid that even today I try to kick my own backside for being such as ass.

'Come up for a coffee then.' Lynn was very serious now. 'I need to talk to someone, and you're nice, you're a good listener.' I really should have been certified there and then, and locked up for life in a home for the feeble-minded, because my mind was clearly unbalanced. I was quite mad. The lovely Lynn was inviting me up for coffee, and I'm sure we both knew that once there it would be inevitable that we would end up in bed together. She needed comforting and I needed sex, and money. Only work would make both possible, to my mind. The whole thing was ridiculous. Opportunity was not so much knocking as hammering at the door, demanding admittance, and here was I passing up an offer that was a gift from heaven.

Lynn brought me down to earth. 'You don't understand women, do you.' It was a statement of fact, not a question. She spoke quietly. 'I need to be held, I feel all alone. I'm frightened.' This was uncharted territory for me. I knew very little about what made women tick, but I knew myself well enough to know that I did not possess it, that certain something that turns them on.

'Look, Lynn,' I said briskly, trying to be businesslike and positive. 'Things will look better in the morning. Next week when I call round we can go out for a drink or something. I'll have more time to spare then.' Lynn shook her lovely head and her hair swung gently,

'Listen, Doug. This is a once in a lifetime offer.' She whispered the words. 'You can have me if you want me.' She paused, and added. 'Don't leave; please don't leave me, not now.' My mind was whirling. This was heavy, heady stuff. I wanted her, but I blew it big time, and sounded as stupid as Highland Donald.

'Lynn, my word is my bond. You can depend on me not to let you down. Your milk and cigarettes will be there in the morning, you'll see.'

'I doubt it,' she said resignedly. 'It really doesn't matter.' As she climbed down from the cab she paused by my driver's window. 'You know something? I only know your Christian name, but you're nice. I wish I had met someone like you sooner.' With that compliment she brushed her lips against my cheek and was gone.

As I knew I would be, I was kept busy for the next several hours running up and down the Queensferry Road, and all points off it to the right and left. As I had promised, I bought and delivered the cigarettes. Although the flats were in a rough area the staircase was brightly lit and my fears of a chance attack there dissipated. I was half-hoping that she would hear me, or that there might be a light on, or sounds of movement in the flat. My pockets were by then replenished by dint of hard labour and I hoped that we might again discuss her 'once in a lifetime' proposition. The milk I dropped off just before five in the morning, as dawn was breaking, and I have to admit that I made more noise than was strictly necessary in the hope that Lynn would be up and about at that ungodly hour. Lynn must have been dead to the world by then, but hope springs eternal and all that. I thought of her constantly and the days could not pass quickly enough. Taxi-driving is a fickle trade and it is hard to resist the raising of a hand. For quite a few days no one seemed keen to visit anywhere off Queensferry Road.

Try as I might, I could not get to Muirhouse until the Thursday. Lynn had been on my mind and I had rehearsed what I would say to her. My thoughts had ranged from a lustful half-hour to a little whitewashed cottage in the country with roses round the door, the smell of freshly baked bread from the oven and the sound of children at play in the flower-filled gardens. Could Lynn possibly be as perfect as I had thought? Had the night played tricks with my memory? I would soon find out, and drove to the door of the flats. The annoying thing was that they all looked the same. I was sure that this was the right one, but what should have been Lynn's windows were covered in whitening. Typical of her I thought, she was probably wallpapering and painting to improve things for the kids. Christmas was only four months away and she would make sure that this year it was an event to remember. I hoped that I could contribute. Perhaps a Santa outfit and a Yo-Ho-Ho as I climbed the stair, sack on back, to distribute toys to the girls and a welcome from Lynn. Then again, when completely sober, Lynn might hardly remember the incident or the offer.

As I bounded up the stairs I was ready for anything, from open arms to a cold shoulder. I could get nothing less than a cup of coffee and a chance to work my charm on her again. If I had to spend a few pounds to entice the delightful Lynn into a warm bed I was ready for that too. In fact it could be a good arrangement. No emotional tie, no responsibility for three growing kids and Lynn on tap; this was any red-blooded man's dream. I rattled the door knocker boldly. What if she had a new man installed? That was the worst of all scenarios, but it could happen, and if it did I was calling only for my outstanding taxi fare. The house had an empty sound. The double tap reverberated back to me so I looked through the letterbox and discovered bare floorboards. She had done a moonlight flit. Just wait until I saw Pete Chalmers. Conned again Douglas! But I was in Highland Donald's position and desperate not to let go. I thought I'd leave a note, in the hope that she would get it first- or second-hand. The note would be bland and non-committal in case it fell into the wrong hands. If hubby had reappeared ready to compromise that would be the best of all worlds, particularly for Lynn and the kids. I would not want to spoil her chances of happiness. All my short letter stated was my name and the cab office telephone number. A slight noise behind me made me start and I whipped round to find the resident of the facing flat appraising me from behind her half-opened door.

'Can I be of any assistance?' She lisped in a soft Highland burr. I suddenly felt very foolish since I had no idea of Lynn's surname, nor was I certain that this was the correct address. Even the name Lynn could have been a convenient alias.

'I'm looking for the young lady who lives here. I think she's called Lynn, but I'm not sure. She has three little girls.' I was hedging my bets.

'Oh dear, did you no' hear?' Her voice was filled with concern. 'It was Saturday morning. We got such a fright. The wee lassies found her. She had put her heid in the gas oven.'

20

MOIRA'S RETURN

Whether I missed him or he avoided me is unimportant, but it was more than two weeks before I saw that unmistakable head movement bobbing towards me again. Several cabbies had reported that an odd-looking student had been trying to find me. From his opening words, it was clear that he did not think the delay in our meeting was worthy of comment.

'I told you I wass a man of my word.' I decided to remind him that he had agreed to meet me two weeks earlier when, most importantly, he was to pay his outstanding dues. There was no apology for keeping me waiting. I had almost, but not quite, written off the fare that he owed. It was a Thursday evening, the night before the great unwashed got paid, and the taxi business was slack. To my pleasant surprise Donald was actually holding the thirty shillings in his hand. My attitude changed and he was received with warmth and even enthusiasm.

'There you are, chust like I promised,' announced Donald, as he proffered the delayed payment. My annoyance had instantly subsided.

'How's your love life with the delectable Moira?' I enquired, more to torment him than anything else. He had no sense of humour and his face clouded over as he became very serious while he informed me.

'I haff seen nothing of her at all and I am very worried about it. I fear that somet'ing terrible might have happened to her. If your taxi hiss free perhaps we could go and look for her together.' I quickly broke the news to Donald that in my experience nothing on earth was free, and certainly not my taxi.

'No, no,' he protested. 'You haff a business to run and I am not suggesting that you take me round and about without payment, but I'm sure you haff experience of going into pubs and finding people and t'ings like that.'

I was keen to explain some of the facts of low life as seen from the driver's seat of a taxi to Donald, but unfortunately he was a real sobersides and I did not know how to broach the subject. If he was so enthusiastic to experience sex games with Moira, then a straightforward cash offer might well be accepted. Our Yankee cousins were undoubtedly getting it for free, so it could be worth a try. In economic terms it could prove to be a much less expensive route to sharing a bed with her than the one he was pursuing. Somehow, I felt that Donald would faint away at such a suggestion. The other consideration that stayed my hand was that I would do myself out of a taxi fare if he became sensible. As a fine fellow, I was once again appointed as his runner, and at my suggestion we did a tour of the haunts frequented by what we in the trade quaintly referred to as Yankee meat. After some fruitless but nice meter-increasing miles of searching we, or rather I, found her in the most likely place: the International Bar. This time she was distinctly unimpressed at the prospect of seeing Donald again.

'I don't want to see him,' she protested vehemently. 'He's a dirty bastard. Do you know what he did that last time when you talked me into seeing him?' My memory was playing tricks, as I distinctly remembered words like 'darling, I missed you' and 'kiss, kiss' and other terms and acts of endearment. She blustered on. 'The filthy sod actually tore the bottom out of his trouser pocket so that I could touch him up on the way to Richard Shops. He's a real creep, is that one.' I had to agree that Donald was indeed a creep, with disgusting habits, but in some ways enterprising and lucky too, even if it had cost him a few pounds. I had been driving and watching them sitting close together, but his enterprising tailoring alterations had escaped my notice. Moira was determined that as far as she was concerned Donald was a non-person. How they had originally met was never explained.

There is only one way to deliver bad news, and that is to tell it as it is. Bert used to say that the preferred method of the plod when breaking the news of the sudden death of a Mr Bloggs would be to address the lady who answered the door with, 'Are you the widow Bloggs?' A refinement to this was in response to the reactions of the new widow. If she fell into the arms of the PC crying her eyes out she was worth a follow-up visit after about two weeks. By this time she would, with up to three years of her former husband's salary in the bank and the mortgage paid off by the insurance company, have become a fairly wealthy woman. The pangs of loneliness would be rising and the thoughts that her sex life had prematurely ended would make falling into those same strong arms again a natural response.

So I told Donald that his love life as far as the delightful Moira was concerned was kaput and over. He took it badly.

'It hiss the drink that hass got hold of her I am t'inking,' he declared. 'Poor wee lassie. She loves the drink more than she loves me and it hiss sad.' That was it over as far as I was concerned. This philosophical attitude was not shared by our Donald. I knew that drink was not a player in this particular game but held my tongue. Highland Donald had other ideas. 'We must,' he suddenly cried in his anguish, 'fight fire with fire I am t'inking. Now listen.' He addressed me directly. 'Be a good fellow and go back in and see Moira and tell her I haff a bottle of whisky in the car.' This approach would have guaranteed success if his target had been Methy Maggie but was obviously doomed to failure with the delicious Moira. 'You just go into the bar and tell her I haff a bottle of good whisky and she will come running just as nice as you like.' Donald had greater faith in the power of the spirit than I had. Completely against my better judgement, I trailed back into the International to speak with the doe-eyed Moira. I started with an apology.

'I'm really sorry, Moira, but I promised that pillock that I would bring you one last message. He says that he has a good bottle of whisky in the taxi with your name written on it.' Wonders really never do cease and for the first time Moira showed a flicker of interest. 'I've not seen it myself but he swears he's got it for you.' I was covering my back in case the cretin was lying. I then gave Donald an endorsement. 'He has paid his dues and seems to be loaded.' The last bit was pure invention, but it worked like a charm.

'All right,' elected Moira without the slightest hesitation. 'I'll come out and see him, but you stick around, right!' I saved my breath and failed to remind her of how badly she had treated me the last time we had met. The pair of us crossed the road to meet the doleful Donald. Moira had missed her vocation, because she was a born actress with an excellent memory.

'Donald, darling, where have you been?' she purred. I could hardly believe my ears as without a blink or a blush she purred on. 'That afternoon Richard Shops were shut and I was so keen not to disappoint you that I went all over the place to try to find some "you-know-whats" that were suitable. I got some and they're in your favourite colour, black, and they're fabulous, just wait until you see me in them because they'll blow your mind.' This time the glass division stayed open and I had a ringside seat. It was an incredible performance. Donald responded like one of Pavlov's dogs.

'I haff a bottle of whisky for you.' As Donald made this declaration a foxy look flashed across his features.

'Give it me then. If it's mine give it here.' This was an icy command from Moira and I wondered if she had perhaps trained as a dominatrix. She certainly had Donald on a leash. Donald's response proved that he was a pillock of the very first water. With a flourish he produced what he obviously thought was his ace in the hole. The open sesame to sensuous delights – a Bell's miniature!

'What's that?' demanded Moira in a voice that convinced me

that her hobby was correcting naughty former public school-boys. 'What is that miserable little object?' I was listening for the swish of the cane. 'Do you mean to say that you have dragged me across the road from a warm pub to a freezing taxi and that's all you have to offer me?' Donald cringed in fear and blurted out. 'It hiss only to keep you going because I could not be sure I would find you. I haff a lot of money and we can buy a full bottle I am t'inking.'

'Show me.' Moira's demand was voiced in tones that brooked no argument and Donald produced a modest roll of notes. Moira's mercurial mood swung again. 'That's more like it, darling; hand it over and I'll go and get a proper bottle that'll put me in the mood. Then I'll whiz round for my new sussie belt and stockings and we can book a room at the Theatrical Digs in Gilmore Place. Gosh, it's going to be great fun.' It was quite a speech and she effortlessly switched to actress mode. 'You make me really randy, you devil; you've got me excited already, I can hardly wait.' Her hand shot out, not to grab the money as I thought, but lower down, where, for a fleeting instant she massaged the front of his trousers. Then she took the money. 'I'll nip in and get a bottle from the pub and then we can go and collect my things.' With that she dashed from the cab, crossed the road and dived through the side door of the pub. I developed a sinking feeling in my wallet.

'Donald?' I asked very quietly, 'Have you enough on you to pay my fare?' It was a rhetorical question because I knew something that he didn't. Donald was facing the front of the cab but swivelled round in my seat I could see out of the back window. As fast as Moira had entered the side door of the International Bar she had exited from the front door and rounded the corner into Brougham Place. I addressed the dreamy-faced Donald again.

'Have you got enough to settle the fare?' He was not really with it.

'No, I haff not until Moira comes back. But there is enough to book the room and pay you off and everyt'ing.' I wished that

I had his confidence. We waited, and then we waited some more until Donald became anxious. Worry lines were beginning to trace their way across his face when he spoke. 'She hiss a silly girl is Moira. I bet she has gone to collect her t'ings on foot when we could easily have gone for them in the taxi.' This young man was at university so how could he be so dumb? I broke the bad news to him.

'Donald.' I spelled it out to him. 'MOIRA – HAS – GONE – AWAY – WITH – YOUR – MONEY – AND – MY – FARE.' Donald went, as the saying goes, white at the gills and then turned an interesting shade of puce. Puce, for those who do not know it, is the colour you get when you squash a fly. He looked every bit as sick as he must have felt but he had still not learned his lesson.

'Maybe she hass got into company and cannot get away.' His straw clutching was of Olympic standard but his voice lacked conviction. 'Yes, that will be it, so be a good fellow and go in and get her.'

'Donald, do you still not understand? She's done a runner. In the side door and out of the front one. Put it down to experience, but be sure to bring me my two pounds as soon as you can.'

'Maybe she hass been run over or somet'ing. You hear about such t'ings'. It was the last despairing plea from the supreme optimist with the long sad face. We had a few more words at a penny a minute which I might or might not get paid for. He confessed that he had pawned his kilt and other items in a desperate effort to bed the elusive Moira. The only addict in the sorry saga was Donald himself, a slave to unrequited lust. I was pretty hopeless with women but Donald was a volunteer sucker. I doubt if Moira would have tried it on with any normal person. A guy who lacks the confidence to enter a public bar in pursuit of the woman he lusts after must have been an irresistible target.

Technically speaking, she had perhaps broken the law, but it would be very difficult to lay charges if the torn-out pocket were to be produced in evidence. Donald repeated his formulae that he wass a man of honour and that his word wass his bond and all that twaddle. This time, however, he walked home. His parting remark proved that he had heard and learnt nothing at all.

'I hope nothing hass happened to Moira, because she could be lying injured in the hospital, I am t'inking.' That was Donald's trouble. He did too much t'inking.

21

M AND S G

Drunks are a constant bugbear for taxi drivers. They can range from the most amusing companions to seriously dangerous individuals. Junkies were an unknown quantity and practically nonexistent in the mid 1950s. Most cabbies, when the Edinburgh pubs closed sharply at ten, would carry a supply of whisky and cigarettes in their cabs. Such goodies were sourced from the American Air Base at Kirknewton. Being nicely outside the city limits the fare was negotiable and generally agreed at one pound twenty-five pence, but either a bottle of Canadian Club or 200 Pall Mall cigarettes were equally acceptable. The Canadian whiskey was supplied in 40-ounce bottles and there was a steady demand on the streets for it at two pounds a bottle. Despite its being an acquired taste and discounted by Scotch whisky drinkers until they had nothing else, it mixed well with cola and did the business, so it sustained many a late-night party.

There is a definite pecking order among drunks. Gin and It or G and T are top shelf. An LO, aka a leg opener, is a Brandy and Babycham, and although not quite top-drawer is most effective and therefore very popular. Rapidly descending through flat-rib beer and porter is found the Wee Heavy and Barley Wine merchants. They are usually well on the way to the bottle in the bag, usually British fortified wine, favoured by the late-night round-the-bonfire crowd. All of the above look down on methylated spirit drinkers, since even at this level there is a division. White meths drinkers find it hard to come by and consider it medicinal, while the imbibers of the blue variety are suicidal. Meths drinkers exude a peculiar and unpleasant odour. Rock bottom is the partaker of M and S G, the acronym for milk and stair gas. The reason that he or she is considered to be the lowest of the low is because they imbibe for free, usually alone, and this is considered unacceptable. Having drunk their fill they spend their recovery period unconscious, which is decidedly unsociable.

An explanation may be required, and is issued with a very serious health-risk warning. It is a particularly Scottish drink. As Mrs Beeton, the world's first serious cookery writer, might have said, first find your tenement, and in seeking it out opt preferably for an older one. Those built in the 1870s are best, and the age can often be verified by an etched stone on an outside wall. For English or overseas readers, tenements are tall buildings providing accommodation for a goodly number of families and found throughout Scotland. This recipe is no reflection on the residents.

Having found your tenement, mount the stairs until you locate an unclaimed bottle of milk sitting forlornly on a doorstep. Take charge of the bottle and, for beginners, the half-pint size should prove adequate. Remove the protective shield from the gaslight that illuminates the staircase by day and night, as such buildings are invariably dark places, and push the bottle onto the gas outlet in the same movement as a landlord pushing a glass under a spirit dispensing optic and allow the coal gas to bubble through the milk. This action, having extinguished the gas lighting, means that guesswork comes into play, but a few minutes of activity should suffice. Drink the milk containing the gas.

This beverage was famous throughout Scotland, and when and if you recovered you would have experienced no pain or discomfort whatever. Total oblivion. You could of course be dead, which may be much the same thing. Fortunately or unfortunately, according to your point of view, coal gas is no longer used to illuminate buildings – unless you know otherwise. If you do know of a suitable building and the word gets about then twitchers, not, I'm afraid, of the feathered-friend admiring variety, but grey-faced men and women with shaky hands, will flock to the site to indulge in an almost forgotten Scottish ritual.

Indeed, in most Scottish cities young men will freely admit to having been 'gassed' last night. Don't be alarmed, because it simply means that he was drunk and the term has now passed into the language through common usage.

This book was intended to be amusing, but it has become, without intent, educational.

22

GOLDBAUM

A certain Dale Carnegie wrote a book called *How to Win Friends and Influence People*, and it not only made him a millionaire when it became an international bestseller, it changed him into a world-famous guru with adoring clients hanging on his every word. He changed many lives for the better throughout the world. Some people are lucky like that. On the other hand take Mr Goldbaum, whom no one has ever heard of; Dale Carnegie was not in his league as far as face-to-face success is concerned. Mr Goldbaum had a great influence on my life and my modest success, the villa in the south of France where I moor my 100-foot yacht, the racehorses and the good life I owe in part to the early training in sales techniques that he afforded me. His influence first put my foot firmly on the ladder of success.

I had always fancied the lifestyle of a sales representative as seen from the front seat of a taxi. The expense accounts and the wining and dining of clients in the very best hotels had a certain appeal for someone forced to use the 'greasy spoon' in the Caledonian Station. For most people the idea of being your own boss gives status and freedom of action, but working for yourself in reality as a taxicab owner meant that every client was your employer. In addition, never-ending lists of bills and accounts were constantly falling overdue. I was ready to move on to better things, but how to get started? A first job in sales was hard to land. There were plenty of positions being advertised which offered a good starting salary, but the required qualifications were daunting. Fluency in two languages and a willingness to spend six months abroad each year, plus years of experience, with an upper age limit of 25. Where on earth did they find such people? Unless they were the sons of the bosses. Then a job that was different was listed in the *Edinburgh Evening News*, and it leapt off the page at me. It was exactly what I had been looking for.

UNIQUE OPPORTUNITY

International Domestic Utilities market leader requires trainee Marketing Executives immediately. £75 per week salary for on target earnings. Full corporate training programme so no experience necessary. Own car and telephone, leads supplied. No cold calling. Bonded position RING NOW for early interview . . . WAVerlay 2345.

This was meant for me, and the prospect of £75 a week starting salary had '£' signs dancing before my eyes. A good week's driving earned me about fifteen pounds, and apart from the unsociable hours a large percentage of this was swallowed up by little luxuries like food and drink. Instead of the cab keeping me, I seemed to be keeping the cab. Its needs always took precedence over my own. With £75 for working Monday to Friday I could drive the cab at weekends and earn another £10 easily. With an income of £85 a week I wouldn't call the king my cousin. Armed with a handful of coppers, I rushed to a telephone box only to find that the number seemed to be permanently engaged. It was clear that competition for the job was going to be fierce. Perhaps this was a first test to challenge the resolve of the applicants, so I persevered and eventually my call was answered. To judge from the background noises, business must be booming. They must have been impressed by the sound of my voice, because following a surprisingly short conversation, during which it was stressed that a deposit of £50 in cash would be required until my bond could be arranged, I was granted an interview the following morning. The venue was a small hotel in Abercromby Place, and the time of my interview ten o'clock.

On arriving in the morning resplendent in my RAF-badged blazer and tie I was surprised to discover fifteen or sixteen others milling about in the small foyer of the rather down-at-heel pension. A boot boy wearing a green pinafore greeted each new arrival without enthusiasm, and when not ticking names off a list was kept busy polishing the brass items dotted about the place. During this waiting period we appraised each other, wondering who was likely to be successful and forming little groups where we passed the time in meaningless chitchat. How would the lucky few be chosen? If smart appearance was the criterion, I was in with a shout.

Eventually, a good fifteen minutes behind schedule, we were ushered into what was obviously the dining room of the hotel. Chairs and tables littered with breakfast crumbs were haphazardly arranged round the room and to one side a green baize-covered table dominated the arena. The boot boy invited us to arrange chairs in rows in front of this table and told us to be seated. Like sheep we obeyed, and waited expectantly for something to happen. I had expected a face-to-face affair and the idea of a group interview was foreign to my experience. Stragglers were still appearing and by ten-thirty there must have been twenty-five or more of us sitting demurely in serried ranks.

The boot boy, having removed his pinny, stood by the door and, reading from a printed card in a monotone voice, he made his announcement:

'Ladies and gentlemen, I am happy and proud to introduce you to the sales development manager for the world's leading home hygiene appliance manufacturer – Rokoko International – Mr C K Goldbaum!' With that the double door burst open and Claude Kitchener Goldbaum trotted in and made his impressive entrance. There was no fanfare, no spotlights and no one had told us to applaud, so it was a bit of an anticlimax. Mr Goldbaum appeared not to notice. He believed in making an impact and obviously thought that his appearance represented the epitome of sophistication. We in our innocence thought so too. We sat to attention, waiting for the great man to speak. His suit was very shiny, not from wear but by design, and was the first mohair clothing that any of us had seen. He was clearly Jewish, well-fed, and his hair, though thinning, was in a crew-cut style. A black shoelace with a red stone inset where a knot should have been was worn instead of a tie. His fingers were adorned with lumpy silver rings and his Timex watch had red stones instead of numerals. He was clearly an all-American boy. Only his parents' mistake in naming him after Lord Kitchener stopped him cheating on his age.

'Goomorning, gennelmen.' He hailed us. 'My name is Goldbaum and I guess I owe youse all an apology for keeping youse waiting for a minute or two. In our business punk-u-alidy is dead important. Anyway, I'm here and I'm going to tell youse all about the Rokoko, the best vacuum cleaner in the world, which is going to make some of youse lucky guys rich.'

His audience, who had never heard of Rokoko International and had no interest in selling vacuum cleaners door-to-door, met this statement with blank indifference. Mr Goldbaum was unabashed and pressed on.

'My job is to recruit and train the best of youse guys and turn them into the highest paid and the most professional sales force in the Uni'ed Kingdom.' His accent was unique, with lots of Americanese and even more Glasgow patois, with the Gorbals being the source at a guess. 'We is not in the business of selling vacuum cleaners door-to-door, no sirree, we is in the hygiene business, an' I have just came back from a very successful campaign in the US of A.' As he delivered this earth-shattering piece of news he beamed at his audience and checked to see how impressed we were. The effect was spoiled by the inevitable joker in the pack who whispered, sotto voce, 'Aye, the other side o' Airdrie.' Mr Goldbaum pretended not to have heard and carried on, insincerity oozing from every pore.

'Youse are the finalists, selected from thousands of applicants, so youse are the lucky ones. But before we go any further I must run over the terms of the advert-ise-ment what we placed in the papers. Now this is dead important: has youse all got auto-mobiles? Hands up anybody what has not got a motor?' Three unfortunates raised their hands and were immediately asked to leave the meeting.

'Sorry, lads,' sympathised Claude Kitchener, 'but without a car youse can't do this job so youse will have to leave.' We were shocked at the ruthlessness that was obviously part and parcel of this business. The nervous chap sitting on my right put up a tentative arm.

'I've only got a van; will that be OK?' He sounded as if he was grovelling a bit.

'Well, yes, I guess it is accep'able because you can always hide it roond a corner when you make a call. Be sure to buy a new car with your first pay cheque.'

This made us sit up, which was exactly what the wily Mr Goldbaum had intended it would. A new car that quickly was what we all wanted and I said nothing about having a taxi.

'Now listen out all of youse, especially them at the back. Our unique training programme will turn youse into world-class salesmen, and it starts right *now*!' Mr Goldbaum came from behind the table and stood in front of us. 'Let me have a look at your fingernails and the toecaps of your shoes.' The demand and tone reminded me of a sergeant-major. Goldbaum, as he carried out the inspection, repeated his personal mantra: 'We is in the home hygiene business and if youse have turned up for an interview with dirty fingernails or dirty shoes youse are nae use tae me nor to Rokoko International.' Following this vetting another half-dozen were cast into outer darkness. The class was reducing in size but the quality was improving.

'I shall now,' he announced, pausing to build up the atmosphere, 'unveil our trade-smashing product.' Mr Goldbaum reached under the green baize and produced two boxes. One was six inches square by a foot long and the second a foot square by a yard long. He also unrolled an advertising poster about three feet by four feet and pinned it to the wall. It illustrated a very glamorous lady in a frilly apron smiling in satisfaction and using a gleaming cylinder vacuum machine fitted with a long hose with a nozzle attachment. Underneath in large lettering was the legend: THE NEW ROKOKO – THE LITTLE GEM – THE HOUSEWIFE'S FRIEND and in a twelve-inch diameter eye-catching roundel the price was displayed – Only 5 Guineas – cash.

To say that the unveiling caused a favourable reaction is an understatement; genuine gasps of amazement were heard. No wonder you could earn £75 a week, because it would be easier than shelling peas distributing beauties like these. Housewives would be queuing up to part with their cash. The doubting Thomases amongst us who had been wary about the prospect of putting down a £50 deposit were readily reassured. Mr Goldbaum beamed a satisfied smile because he now had our undivided attention, and he knew it.

'I will now let youse into a little secret. Youse will never guess what I done last week?' Blank stares greeted his words. 'I delivered twelve Rokokos to the Hoover fak'try in Glasgow. I had to go at night, under cover like, since it had to be hush-hush. Their cleaning staffs was on strike and they was demanding Rokokos before they would go back to work. They would nae ha'e a Hoover in the place. You see, there's a thing cried brand accep'ance, and youse all know that everybody cries any vacuum cleaner a Hoover, even our Rokoko! Our machine is more better than theirs is but they is still the number ones and we is the number twos.' Whether the scatological reference was intended or not was unclear, but it was pounced on by his budding sales force and Mr Goldbaum thought we were smiling with happiness for him and his coup. That said, we did believe him because this 'Little Gem' was a real trade topper without any doubt.

'I will now demonstrate the "Little Gem".' He then unpacked the smaller box to reveal a miserable little object that bore no relation to the artist's impression on the poster. The cylinder was nine inches long by one and a half inches in diameter. Attached was a half-inch diameter hose about a foot long and the whole thing was mounted on fragile coat-hanger type metal runners. On reflection one had to admit that, apart from the artistic liberties taken by the artist, there was a vague similarity between the two images. That the lovely lady in the frilly apron was a Lilliputian had been overlooked. The perspective was designed to fool everyone, and hearts dropped into boots.

Mr Goldbaum, ignoring the change in atmosphere, plugged it into the mains. For a full half-minute nothing happened, then the poor little thing coughed, shivered, and then spluttered and wheezed into life. For all the world it looked like a premature baby vacuum cleaner in need of an intensive care unit and an incubator. The little mite continued to struggle for life as Mr Goldbaum thrust the nozzle into an ashtray to demonstrate the power of the Little Gem. It half-heartedly stirred the ash around a little for a moment or two and then asthmatically puffed some of the lighter ash fragments into the air. This all proved too much for the Little Gem and in a tragic fit of coughing and gasping it died. There was an embarrassed silence from the audience.

'I know what youse is thinking,' shouted the clairvoyant Mr Goldbaum, 'but there's a cunning plan behind our sales drive. The hoosewife will have her fiver ready when you call and youse has to go all out tae sell her this wee one. She will DEF-IN-ITE-LY no' want it, but youse has tae go all out tae try tae make her have it. Then youse produce this big belter.' As he said this the larger box was opened, and out slid a magnificent looking machine finished in red and gold, with the legend 'The Rokoko Major' emblazoned on each side.

'We also do it in blue and silver,' shouted the irrepressible Mr Goldbaum over the powerful roar of the machine, now that it was plugged into the electrical socket. It ran with a smooth, powerful humming noise as the air thrashed through the system. When proffered the contents of the ashtray it dragged the detritus across space and did its best to gobble down the tray as well. Small denomination coins were swallowed with a throaty rattle. It was supplied with a range of equipment meant to reach any nook or cranny ever fashioned by man. The instruction leaflet made it clear that with this breakthrough in technology it was possible to spray-paint cars. If the Little Gem was worth five guineas, this monster must be worth ten times as much of anyone's money.

'The price of the big Rokoko Major, gennelmen,' announced Mr Goldbaum, having switched the monster off, 'is a mere thirty-five dollars – I'm sorry, I meant pounds – I forgot where I wiz for a meenit. Only thirty-five guineas. What do youse think of that?'

The effect on the embryo sales force was mixed. None of us had the vaguest notion of the price of a new Hoover upright, or cylinder model for that matter, but it was undeniable that the big Rokoko looked and sounded like excellent value. This was particularly true when compared with the late, unlamented Little Gem.

'But that's not all, gennelmen.' Claude Kitchener held up his hands as if to stem a tide of eager buyers. He was now in full flow. 'The best news of all is that it can be theirs for only five guineas' deposit. Yes sir, five guineas down, and the rest on the "chucky" at fifteen bob a week. Mind how the advert-ise-ment showed a price of only five guineas cash. Well, by now the hoosewife will be ready with her cash because she had promised herself a new vacuum and she will decide to spend it on a Rokoko cleaner. Now do youse grasp the cleverness of the strategy?' Even the dimmest had got the message. 'It's what we in the trade cry switch-selling, and it will make youse all a fortune.' Mr Goldbaum paused for breath.

'Now gennelmen, to carry on with the training. Switch-selling only works if youse try your hardest to sell the Little Gem. A word of warning here. If youse is daft enough to sell it youse is finished with Rokoko because the wee yin costs a fortune to make. Believe it or not, they cost twice as much as the biggie so DO NOT SELL IT. OK?' Mr Goldbaum was now on a roll. 'Now, a quick demonstration on how to sell the Rokoko Major. First of all, compliment the hoosewife on what a clean hoose she has and youse can even say that it's that clean that she disnae need a cleaner at all. Then take oot your hankie.' At this point, Mr Goldbaum whipped a freshly laundered one from his top pocket and placed it like a filter between the attachment and the hose. He switched on the machine and drew the nozzle across the green baize just once. When the handkerchief was removed and examined a black circle of dirt was revealed on the snow-white cloth.

'Show it to the hoosewife,' Goldbaum instructed. 'She will be black affronted. Youse will have done her a favour and showed her what a dirty hoose she is living in. She will be desperate to buy off you, and now here's a few more tips to help youse.' Super-salesman Goldbaum was warming to his task of training. 'Youse should always refer to the hoosewife as the "little woman" if the husband is there, even if she's built like a brick shed. Always remember love is blind. If he is no' in, get her to sign his name on the hire-purchase form.' As if struck by a sudden thought, super-salesman Claude struck his forehead. 'Annurrer word of warning that I forgot to tell youse was, never do the hankie trick twice, or go over a thing twice to show how clean it is now that you've cleaned it. The dirt is in the air and you'll just lose a sale if you do that. And watch it with the drapes. Be very careful, because the suction is that strong that you could pull them doon. Any questions?'

'What's drapes?' This from a fool in the front row.

'Sorry, gennelmen,' gushed the immodest Mr Goldbaum. 'I spend that much time in the States that I forget mysel' at times. Drapes is just curtains. Any more questions?'

'What about the wages? The £75 a week and that?' The whole room was interested in this question but our Mr Goldbaum was quite unfazed.

'We operate what we cry a commission structure,' he confirmed. 'It's the only system accep-able to top professional salesmen. Youse will get five pound and five shillings for every sale. If youse keep busy and sell one in the morning and one in the afternoon and say two at night, youse'll draw a hundred pound-odd a week and have the weekends free to watch the Hearts or the Hibs fitba' teams. It's a great life, is the selling game.'

We nodded our agreement. As fellow salesmen who would be working hard we could appreciate the need to relax at the weekends. Twenty sales a week seemed a reasonable target, and the potential earnings quite breathtaking. Mr Goldbaum continued with his Niagara of advice.

'Don't give nobody a discount except your mothers.' He was all heart, was Mr Goldbaum. 'The five pound deposit you collect is your wages. Any discount youse give away to customers is coming out yer ain pockets.' He then put on a serious face to warn us of some of the pitfalls in a career in domestic sales. 'It will take youse a week or two to get the hang of selling the Rokoko, but youse all look as if youse are star potential to me. Mind, it's very easy to blow it because some of them hoosewifes is man-hungry and they come to the door with their night dresses hingin' open and everything, so watch out.' To most of us this was the final strawberry to the assembled donkeys. Just the incentive we needed to sign up with Rokoko International and get started selling and meeting housewives with open-fronted frocks and be earning right away. Only then, with his eager audience well and truly hooked, did our C K Goldbaum reveal a slight snag.

'Of course, gennelmen, being businessmen yourselfs, you will realise that we at Rokoko International do not know youse from Adam.' The elevation to businessmen was a nice touch and we agreed wholeheartedly. 'Youse could be a bunch of conmen or anything, so youse will have to pay a deposit of fifty pounds against your first Wee Gem and Rokoko Major. Fifty pounds, like we said on the blower. Youse will have it refunded as soon as the insurance company clears youse.'

This sudden announcement caused some fidgeting amongst the remaining hopefuls. Some, who had no doubt expected that it would be some time before they would be recruited, had overlooked this detail. Mr Goldbaum resolutely stood his ground. 'If some of youse cannot find fifty pounds to set up a career then youse are no use to Rokoko International, so I'll invite youse to leave now.' As the cashless left, Mr Goldbaum instantly reclassified them from 'star potential' to 'dem bums'. The class was reduced to seven clean-fingernailed, shiny-toed, £50-in-cash-carrying innocents. The matter of administration was now discussed.

Each morning, Mr Goldbaum would await our arrival at the General Post Office in Waterloo Place. The busy office noises I'd heard on the phone were thus explained. In exchange for each correctly completed hire-purchase form or £31 10s. in cash, he would issue a boxed Rokoko Major from the rear of a huge furniture removal van parked nearby. He also promised to hand out press leads in proportion to sales achieved. Included in our £50 deposit was a vast supply of leaflets that were exact but smaller copies of the misleading poster advertising the Little Gem. These were to be used to leaflet any street from which we had received an enquiry from a newspaper advertisement. Our deposits would be returned at some unspecified date in the future, and the credit check with the unnamed insurance company must have been arranged telepathically, since no forms were completed in that regard. It was all very professional and business-like.

'Now,' enthused the enterprising Mr Goldbaum, 'I'm going to show youse something that is a closely guarded secret. It is beyond price an' worth more'n money. It has took me years to

147

work it out. It is the real secret of successful selling that no' even that Dale Carnegie bloke kens aboot.' He then instructed the survivors to gather their chairs in a circle around the green baize-covered table. With yet another of his unexpected flourishes he produced a candle that he lit and placed in the middle of the table. He drew the curtains, making the room quite dark, and asked us to join hands to complete an unbroken circle. We sat rather apprehensively in a silent circle staring at the candle. Then he whispered, 'I want youse to put oot the candle wi' the concentration o' your unit-ed minds. Really try,' he urged. 'In yer minds visualise it oot. Try your best now, all of us together.' Some of us suspected a trick of some sort, but Claude Kitchener Goldbaum was deadly serious. He chided us, 'Somebody at this table is definitely no tryin' hard enough. Are youse sure the chain is no broken? Are youse all holding hands?' We really tried hard and for a minute the flame sank down, but it recovered and flared up again.

'Youse nearly done it that time,' breathed Mr Goldbaum. 'Just a bit mair effort and we'd have had it oot. Try again, come on and concentrate because youse can do it.'

Despite our best efforts, the candle stayed firmly lit. The flame flickered contentedly at our discomfiture. Svengali Goldbaum would not surrender. He had not risen to the top in Rokoko International by allowing nature to beat him. One final try he urged and we responded, at least I did, I tried like mad. It was all to no avail and eventually Mr Goldbaum stood up and reached across and snuffed out the flame between his dampened finger and thumb.

'That's the final lesson for youse. Youse has seen it with yer own eyes. If you want something to happen it's no good sittin' on yer arses an' thinkin' aboot it. Even thinkin' hard. To make sales youse have got to get up off-of yer backsides and make it happen.'

And so it came to pass that shortly before noon I was to be found walking along Abercromby Place in the company of six others. Each had a Rokoko Major under one arm and a Little Gem under the other and every pocket was stuffed with leaflets and hire-purchase forms to meet the anticipated huge demand. Despite having successfully completed Mr Goldbaum's rigorous training programme I did not feel like a world-class sales representative. With every step away from Mr Goldbaum the umbilical cord of confidence was stretching thinner and thinner. My new-found confidence was gradually draining away, but I was committed to giving the business a try. I had no idea whether or not I could sell Rokoko vacuum cleaners, but Claude Kitchener Goldbaum certainly could. In less than two hours he had sold seven Majors and seven Gems, and pocketed £350 pounds.

Not a bad morning's work!

23

BIG TAM

The four bag-laden gents blinking in the bright afternoon sunshine as they wandered down Picardy Place had been enjoying a heavy lunchtime session in Mather's Bar at the top of Broughton Street. The party had been ended by the landlord insisting that he was entitled to his afternoon break but, fair do's, he had sold them their carry-outs so all was not lost. Even at that time of day, action was possible in the vicinity of the Deep Sea restaurant. They were no doubt heading in that direction when they spotted my cab. By rights I should have ignored them. The Top End rank was just round the corner opposite the Deep Sea but being out of sight of the cabbies loitering there I took a chance and stopped to pick them up.

'Where to, lads?' It was the standard greeting, delivered in a welcoming tone of voice. They climbed into the cab and settled down, taking their time about it. 'Where to, lads?' I repeated, anxious to be away.

'This'll do fine, pal,' was the puzzling reply. By now the four amigos had produced tumblers from their pockets and screwtops from the paper bags and were passing cigarettes and drinks to each other. I felt that I had to make clear just whose cab it was.

'What do you mean, this'll do fine? Where do you want to go? I can't just park here.' They were unfazed.

'Course you can, it's a free country i'ntit, an' the meter's runnin' i'ntit?'

'Come on pal an' ha'e a bevvy wi' us.'

With this kind invitation a screw-top was thrust through the partition and landed in my lap. The four, ignoring me completely, carried on their conversation as though having a party in a taxi were the most natural thing in the world. They were talking about someone called Big Tam. While I worked out what to do to get rid of them I listened in. Within minutes the cab was filled with a smoky fug, making it quite festive, but there was no way they were going to hold a party in my taxi at half-past-three on a sunny afternoon. Not at a penny a minute waiting time they weren't. However, there were four of them and all big lads who were slightly drunk. Discretion was called for. The story continued.

'I'm telling you it's Big Tam. Mind how he used to be a bouncer at the Palais? Well he's in the big time in the filums noo.' I visualised a shaking of heads.

'It canny be Big Tam, he never worked in 'is life.'

'It is so Big Tam but he cries hissel' Sean noo. Mind how he got chucked oot o' the Navy 'cause he had flat feet or sumthin'? Well you should see him jump about in this filum. Ah don't think there's anythin' wrang wi' 'is feet.'

The penny dropped. Being a couple of years younger than the man in question, my only dealings with Big Tam had been in avoiding Connery's corner on the odd visit to the Palais de Danse in Fountainbridge. I had graduated with little honour from Dickson's Dancing Academy, directly opposite where I was now parked. There I had been taught how to request the pleasure from a prospective partner, how to entertain her with small talk as we pounded the floor in strict tempo to records of Victor Sylvester's celebrated orchestra, and how to return the lady to her seat with thanks. At the Palais de Danse the girls were of a different quality. A nod towards the floor was either rewarded by a girl turning her back – a definite no – or, if she were favourably inclined or desperate, her cigarette would be stubbed out and she would move towards the floor with no further acknowledgment. No conversation took place during the dance, but her jaws would constantly move, chewing-gum having replaced the cigarette. When the music stopped she would retire to join her friends. The politeness drummed into us by Mr Dickson was completely lost on the 'wee hairies' as we called the hatless girls who frequented the establishment. The title 'wee hairies' dated back to pre-war days; girls had long since abandoned the wearing of hats, but the name stuck.

Big Tam was employed as one of the dozen or so maroon-coated bouncers required to keep order in the Palais de Danse. Although he was tall enough and had the required muscles, he was not at all keen on the prospect of his undoubted good looks being spoiled by a flying fist. He therefore operated his own gang within the bouncing fraternity. They claimed as their own the far corner of the balcony and as a mark of their power allowed no one to pass. In order to eye up the available talent we timid types had to make long detours to avoid offending his chums. When trouble did flare up, Big Tam directed operations from the rear while his acolytes did his bidding and escorted trouble-makers towards the door to be carted off by Edinburgh's finest.

'Wait till I tell youse,' went on the narrator. 'Do youse mind how he used to swan aboot pullin' the birds at Portobello Pool when he got fixed up as a baths attendant? Well, when the season ends 'n' he gets the push he disnae want tae get another job. He wants tae get back on the dole right away.' I was beginning to enjoy the tale, and in those far-off days no one saw harm in the odd beer for a driver. I decided to sample the screw-top and put off the inevitable confrontation with my clients. 'When he goes tae the brew tae register, the boy behind the counter says tae him, "What's yer trade?" Big Tam was right fly 'n' he says "I'm a life guard." "Oh," says the boy behind the counter, "we don't have much call for lifeguards roond here." So Big Tam kent he was safe. He could draw the dole until the next summer, when he could get took on again at Portobello Pool.'

'If it's him it's the same bloke awright,' confirmed one of the listeners.

'I telt you it was him. It's def-in-ite-ly Big Tam we're talkin' aboot.' There was general agreement that the subject of the discussion was indeed Big Tam Connery. 'Anyroad,' the raconteur continued, competing with the clinking of glasses and the offers of refills from screw-tops. 'The King's Theatre was looking for blokes to walk on as sodgers in the Student Prince or somethin' like that'n' they had to be six feet tall tae fit intae the uniforms that they had, so they rings up the dole office. They did that in every toon that the show went to. Big Tam was right oot o' luck because the boy in the brew looked up jobs under lifeguards, 'cause he had an idea that was sodgers, so he had fund a job for Big Tam. I think he was after Big Tam 'cause they dinnae like blokes they canny get jobs for. You would think it was their ain money they gi'e oot. Anyroad, Big Tam had tae go for an interview or lose his dole money, but it wiz right up his street. Well, you ken he wiz a right show-off. He fancies his chances on the stage, struttin' aboot 'n' that, 'n' he thought he looked great in the uniform 'n' everythin'. Well the big star, whoever she wiz, takes a right shine tae Big Tam 'n' thinks he wiz the bizzness 'n' she makes sure he gets took on. Her husband isnae there, ken what ah mean, so she talks Big Tam intae goin' tae Glasgow with the show when it moves 'n' he stays on right through the tour.

'She was gi'in' him actin' lessons 'n' that, 'n' Big Tam was teachin' her the horizontal tango. Whatever he wiz doin', they say Big Tam was fair knackered; her an aulder woman 'n' aw, ken. He went everywhere wi' the show, so he did, 'n' her pickin' up the tabs until they gets tae London when she had tae gi'e him the bum's rush cause o' her husband 'n' that, ken.' There was a moment or two of silence and an air of what could only be described as sympathy for Big Tam's predicament. As soon as the storyteller had got his second wind he carried on with his narrative. 'Anyroad, Big Tam decides to become a gigolo 'n' soon gets took on by another bird.'

'What's a jiggalo?' queried the dimmest of the quartet.

'A gigolo is a bloke what gets birds tae buy them things like suits 'n' ties 'n' that. She might even let him stay at her hoose.' There was a pause for thought.

'Ah wouldnae mind bein' a jiggalo,' voiced the dimwit.

'Me neither,' came a chorus from the other two. Whether there is a demand for gigolos of limited intelligence, heavily nicotine-stained fingers and sporting two days' beard growth over a grubby shirtfront is open to question, but these three were apparently open to any offers.

'Youse,' judged the storyteller, 'ha'e nae chance. Youse forget that Big Tam is a good-lookin' bloke 'n' although he disnae like work he keep hissel' fit 'n' that.' The trio masked their disappointment very well.

'Maybe we should go tae London like Big Tam. There's mair burds doon there.' Surprisingly, this uncontroversial piece of logic came from the dimwit.

'Anyroad,' the ringleader ploughed on, 'Big Tam's hit the big time noo, 'n' he cries hissel' Sean or James Bond an' has a job in a filum. It just goes tae show you, dun'tit?' The group was unanimous that it did just go to show you, 'dun'tit.' The driver, now that the fable had ended, was cheesed off and wanted a decision.

'Come on now, lads. We can't stay here all day. Where to?' The reply should not have surprised me.

'We don't want to go no place, so we'll just get oot.' At that they gathered their bottles and glasses and got out.

To their credit they paid the few shillings on the meter and a few pence tip for a cab that had not moved an inch. Lured by the smell of frying chips, they drifted off round the corner to savour the delights of the Deep Sea restaurant, where they might just find desperate ladies on the lookout for a gigolo.

24

THE LAVENDER LADIES

The melancholy chimes had been ringing out for some time calling the God-botherers to the churches and chapels in Edinburgh's West End. It must therefore have been a few minutes to eleven when I was dispatched the few yards from the Caledonian Station to the Rutland Hotel. To be late for divine worship is to break the twelfth commandment: some of God's houses would actually close the doors against latecomers, which is hardly a welcoming attitude. A pair of little old ladies were waiting on the steps for me and I was anxious to avoid blame for being tardy.'Good morning, ladies,' I began. 'I've come straight round from the station rank.' They nodded their heads in unison in acknowledgement but appeared to be oblivious of the time. 'It's almost eleven, ladies; where do you want to get to?' My request was ignored as they fussed around each other. Filmgoers would have instantly recognised the type. One was like the little old landlady in the film *The Lavender Hill Mob*, and the other her sister. Dressed identically in lavender and black outfits, they would be, I judged, in their mid-70s, but spry. In the 1950s that was old. Their hats were flowery and both had tiny veils before their eyes. Lilac gloves were worn and matched the outfits perfectly. As they helped each other down the last few steps, the bells stopped tolling and God must have been drumming his fingernails, much as the frustrated driver was doing on the steering wheel of the taxi. They were definitely going to be late. At the bottom of the steps they started a conversation with each other and, giving up on the rush, I dismounted and opened the cabin door for them. There was a lot of 'after you dear' and 'are you all right?' and 'do be careful now' before they were seated and I was back in my own seat. I swivelled round to face them.

'Where to, ladies?' I was still ignored and decided that perhaps they were a little deaf.

'Are you quite comfortable, dear?' each asked of the other as they settled in the back seat. Two sweeter old ladies would be hard to find. They then discussed the fact that they had a very nice young driver. The next topic was the weather: would it rain, or would it clear up? Why not ask the nice young man, the driver, he would be sure to know.

'Driver, do you think it will rain later?' The enquirer turned out to be Miss Abigail. Her sister, Miss Florence, echoed the end of the question . . .

'. . . rain later?'

Before I could get a word in Miss Abigail continued, 'Will the rain come from the east or the west?' The echo caught up . . .

'The west?'

'What do you think, driver?'

'. . . driver?'

They could not have picked a better person to advise them. As a former airman, I had studied cloud formations for a whole hour during basic training only five years before. I therefore spoke with confidence and authority.

'No, nothing to worry about, the wind will keep away the rain and it won't rain before this evening.' They seemed to believe me.

'Did you hear that, Florence?' queried Miss Abigail. 'The young man says it will not rain before this evening, isn't that nice?'

'. . . that nice?'

The echo seemed a permanent fixture in their conversations. Miss Florence had been nodding her head as her sister spoke and in a brave solo conversational flight ventured, 'No rain, good.'

Church was now out of the question and I wondered if they

would decide that it was not worth going, since they were so late and would totter up the stairs back into the hotel leaving me without a fare.

'Where to, ladies?' from a very nice, very patient young taxi driver.

'We think it would be nice to have a drive out into the countryside,' ventured Miss Abigail, clearly the more dominant sister.

'The countryside,' suddenly from Miss Florence.

In the box, which formed part of the seat of LYO350, I had a cache of goodies. A torch and vacuum flask, 200 Pall Mall cigarettes and a bottle of Canadian Club whiskey, and a pristine tartan travelling rug. This was produced with a flourish and the two misses expressed their delight as I spread it over their knees.

'How lovely!' Miss Abigail cried, and a split second later the inevitable repetition from Miss Florence . . .

'Lovely!'

'You decide where we should go, driver; take us somewhere nice.' Miss Abigail had placed a huge responsibility on my shoulders.

'. . . where nice,' followed from Miss Florence.

That was exactly the problem, what was nice for me might not be for two sweet old ladies; I had to think hard. I also had to explain about going outside the city limits in regard to negotiated fares. Sunday is normally very quiet and I was happy to agree to five pounds for the hire, whatever the time or miles involved. Miss Abigail confirmed it.

'Five pounds.'

Miss Florence affirmed, '. . . five pounds.'

That made ten pounds in total, but as it turned out I was delighted with five pounds in the end.

Edinburgh on that Sunday morning was like a Flag Day in Aberdeen, the streets deserted by pedestrians. From the alternatives that I suggested they chose to drive south. They lived by the sea, so would enjoy the chance to admire some previously unexplored countryside.

'You will drive slowly?' Miss Abigail gently cautioned me.

'. . . slowly?'

I was becoming so used to the echo that I hardly heard it now.

'We want to see everything that we can but we're afraid of speed. We were in an accident once in Father's car and that's why we like to be careful'

'. . . careful.'

It struck me that the accident that they were in probably involved running over the man with the red flag walking in front of Father's early boneshaker, but I said nothing. The weather conditions were what might be called fresh. From time to time gusts of wind rocked the cab as we drove south. High in the watery blue sky rain clouds were skudding along, driven by prevailing winds. My prediction that the rain would hold off might come true. The two misses were snug in the back, the glass partition was wide open, and we held agreeable and informative talks.

'We own a small hotel,' stated Miss Abigail, clearly the more garrulous of the pair.

'. . . hotel.'

'In bracing Bridlington,' she continued.

'. . . ington.' They laughed simultaneously at their little joke.

'This is the kind of weather we're used to, it suits us fine.'

'. . . us fine.'

I don't know if Miss Abigail heard or noticed her sister's constant, and to me extremely annoying, habit of repeating the end of her every sentence. When they spoke to each other it didn't happen. Perhaps it was Miss Florence's way of being part of conversations when her sister was around. That apart, they were lively company, considering their advanced years, and must have been popular debutantes in their day. They were perfect examples of the thousands of little old English ladies whose marriage prospects had been blighted by the Great War, or so I surmised. Spinster daughters of the landed gentry now forced to supplement their fixed-interest annuities in as genteel a manner as possible, perhaps converting the family pile into a select hotel. I drove steadily and carefully, as instructed, and they seemed to be enjoying their jaunt as I pointed out the various interesting landmarks and explained their significance. Roslin is a pretty little village and I thought it might be worth a visit. It is also far enough out of town to have justified a five-pound fare. As we entered the village a chorus from the back suggested that we might stop at a hotel for some tea or refreshment of some sort, and it seemed an excellent idea.

The archaic licensing laws in Scotland at that time decreed that on a Sunday alcohol could only be served to bona fide travellers. The inevitable result was a mass migration of thirsty Scots each Sabbath across the closest county boundary. They could then sign the hotel register with a clear conscience and slake their raging thirsts. Roslin was one such destination. As noon, the legal opening hour, neared, cars, vans, motorcycles, bicycles and foot-sore pedestrians converged on the village to establish their credentials and qualify for much-needed refresh- ments. As a result of this unforeseen circumstance, instead of the quiet wayside retreat that I had had in mind for the ladies, the joint was jumping. I explained this to them, but they said it was fine and that they would find the change interesting. I helped them out of the cab and, after we had signed the visitors' book, led them inside. For two ladies who ran a hotel they seemed strangely diffident and unsure of themselves in such surroundings. I herded them to a quiet corner table, where we sat admiring the decor for some time before a harassed waitress arrived to take our order. Then the pantomime began in earnest.

'What would you like, Florence? Would you like a pot of tea or would you prefer some coffee?'

For once there was no echo, perhaps thoughts of food and refreshment filled the void in Miss Florence's mind. 'I'm not sure, Abigail, what do you think?'

Miss Abigail ignored her sister's request and pressed on, 'Would you like a fancy with it or something more substantial?'

'I don't really know, Abigail.' It was stalemate. The waitress lost patience.

'I'll leave you the menu and the wine list and come back.' And she shot off.

Miss Florence had a flash of inspiration and for once took the initiative. 'What about the young man?' Turning to me she enquired. 'What would you like?' At that moment a twinkle appeared in her eye and she added. 'Perhaps you would like something stronger than tea?'

'How silly of me,' agreed Miss Abigail. 'I should have thought of that.' Turning to me she enquired. 'Would you like a beer?'

A second voice added, '. . . beer?' The echo was back, and at this rate the hotel would be closed before we were served, so I agreed at once.

'A lager and lime, please.' So that was one part of the order decided. I also suggested that they have a sherry or something while they examined the luncheon menu. They thought this a wonderful idea and all that remained was for them to make up their minds as to the aperitif they would like. I should have known better. It slowed things down rather than speeded them up. I had the drinks list and read out the ones I thought suitable for the ladies. Dry or sweet sherry, Babycham, a snowball, a warming Cherry Heering, even port with or without lemonade. Everything I mentioned was discussed and considered, and finally, in an agony of indecision, rejected. The incongruity of a snowball at this time of year caused the ladies some restrained mirth. The waitress from across the room looked at me expectantly and acknowledged my shake of the head. In an inspired moment I suggested a gin and tonic.

'Gin and tonic. I've heard of that. Is it nice?'

'. . . nice?' queried Miss Florence.

'Would that be what you call a long drink?' asked Miss Abigail.

I made my quip over the inevitable echo, 'It can be as long as you like!' In response to the blank stares I explained that the amount of tonic decided the length of the drink. I could hardly believe that anyone could live that long without knowing that. What kind of life did they lead?

All being agreed, and in the absence of the waitress, a large denomination note was passed to me, I made my way to the bar, where I was quickly served. By the time I had downed an inch of my lager and lime the ladies' tumblers were empty. They were delighted with my recommendation.

'This is very nice indeed,' enthused the A and F chorus. 'Very nice indeed.'

'Just like lemonade, nice and fizzy,' was Miss Abigail's opinion.

'. . . and fizzy,' confirmed her sister. And emboldened by the alcohol Miss Florence made a request. 'I'd like another of these Gee and Tee things. I like it, it's nice.' Since the statement was made by Miss Florence there was no echo. I had not mentioned the expression, and I wondered where she had picked it up. That first gin had transformed Miss Florence and she was taking the lead for a change, and liking it. By the time I was on my second lager they had disposed of five or six gins each. I thought that I had better advise caution.

'Ladies, gin is known as mother's ruin because it is stronger than it tastes, it really is.' Apart from being a little more loquacious, the gins had seemingly left them unaffected. Perhaps the landlord added holy water on Sundays. Some food was required, to act as blotting paper, just in case. The waitress appeared and I waved her over. She obviously was only part-time staff and probably worked in the post office during the week because she had clearly been post office-trained.

'Kitchen's closed,' she announced peremptorily and flounced off. I thought that I might be able to buy some sandwiches and went off in pursuit of the landlord. I was unsuccessful and when I returned to the table I was surprised to discover that both ladies were sitting behind large glasses filled to the brim with the smoky blue nectar.

'This gin is very nize,' announced Miss Abigail.

'. . . nizzzze,' hiccupped Miss Florence. Clearly, it was time to go. Before we left they insisted that I make a purchase of Gordon's gin to take home to Bridlington, since they did not think it was available south of the border. I paid, on their behalf, the outrageous hotel price for a bottle to the reluctant landlord. They agreed that they might have a glass as a nightcap that night back at the Rutland Hotel. They were also agreed, as they said in harmony that, 'This gin stuff izs really nize.'

I carefully walked them back to the taxi, and apart from them both walking as if on eggshells, they coped remarkably well with their unaccustomed liquid lunch. I tucked them up in the travelling rug on the back seat and for safety's sake I placed the green bottle between them and we set off back to the city. The return journey was in complete contrast to the outward leg. Silence reigned supreme as I carefully and slowly drove directly to the West End. It had been a good trip as far as business was concerned. A couple of lagers, a change in routine, good company and the prospect of five pounds. It worked out at more than a pound an hour, a very welcome change to my usual Sunday routine. Yes, life was good, life was good. My God, I had caught the repetition disease from Miss Florence. I glanced in my little mirrors and they had their heads together, probably dozing gently. In time I drew up outside the hotel smoothly, climbed down, and went to assist my passengers to alight.

'Ladies, ladies,' I cooed. 'We're here, home at the hotel.'

From the taxi a voice exclaimed, 'Piss off!'

Before I could react a second voice instructed, 'Piss off yourself!'

Clearly they were unused to having their post-prandial slumbers disturbed.

As a shell-shocked young taxi driver leaned forward to undrape the travelling rug from their knees, an empty gin bottle fell to the floor and rocked gently. At that instant I made one of my famously accurate predictions for the future. I forecast some little local difficulties. Miss Florence lurched through the door, pushing me aside, and tripped over the running board. She did not fall, but tottered forward until she met the wall where she stood facing it, transfixed. Miss Abigail, anxious not to be left in the cab alone, made a move as I turned to attend to her sister, and cannoned into me. She executed a gentle pirouette before sitting down on the second step of the hotel. She lay rather then fell back but unfortunately her legs remained splayed open, giving the curious and startled passers-by an unrestricted view of her trendy, below-the-knee, lilac bloomers. She then appeared to doze off into a trance-like sleep. The commotion made Miss Florence turn round and at that point her legs gave out and she slid, back to the wall, very slowly and gracefully down it. As she did so her hat, and her hair, moved forward until her hairline was just above her eyebrows. She settled in a sitting position on the pavement, legs outstretched before her, but in a much more modest state than Miss Abigail.

The nice young taxi driver did not know what to do next. His fares were as far down as they could get and therefore in no danger of falling and injuring themselves. Naturally enough, on a Sunday afternoon the stout doors of the hotel were closed fast, and urgent ringing of the bell did not summon a response for some time. The driver had made three or four runs up and down the half-dozen steps before the odd-job man appeared. Between us we restored Miss Abigail to a state of decency. Neither of us was keen to be seen with our hands anywhere near those elasticated nightmares. We were witnesses for each other and between us lifted her, struggled up the steps and deposited her in an armchair in the reception area. On our second journey, with Miss Florence, a shoe fell off onto the steps and we deposited her beside her sister, who was now snoring loudly, mouth wide open, false teeth clattering with each intake of breath. I tried to shove Miss Florence's hair and hat further back on her head but they seemed to be held fast in the forward position by a construction of pins. I dashed out again to retrieve the missing shoe and thought of myself as Prince Charming. But where was

Cinderella? Shocking as the incident was, it was made much worse for me by the aggressive comments and argumentative remarks being passed by my two sleeping beauties. The colourful language of the two sweet old ladies in their sleep had to be heard to be believed. I don't know if it would have made a stevedore blush, but it had me swooning and reaching for the sal volatile. I left a short note of apology for Kathleen, the receptionist-cum-barmaid, and made good my escape.

When I called the next afternoon in search of my dues, it was to find that the two sweet old ladies had gone; the birds had flown the coop. They had cut short their holiday and returned to bracing Bridlington. As far as I was concerned they may not have been all that sweet, but they proved themselves ladies. Despite all that had happened, they had remembered to leave my fiver fare, and a generous tip as well.

25

JO-JO

It was in vogue for a time for girls to adopt boys' names. There was a Johnny and a Frankie, a Bobby and a Sam. Charlie and Freddie also spring to mind. Not that there was anything mannish about any of them, and they were certainly not women trying to act as men or anything like that. In fact, I don't think lesbianism had been invented at that time; I'm pretty sure it hadn't. One of the most attractive by far was a girl with the unlikely appellation of Jo-Jo. She was just short of six feet tall, went in and out in all the right places, and was very particular about the bits that showed. Her teeth were Oxodol white and her jet-black hair was always under control. She was determined to become a GI bride and live in the sun in California where, once she had passed her driving test, she would drive a big car and have a swimming pool and perhaps even be discovered by a movie mogul. She never wondered what on earth a guy who had all he claimed he had at home was doing serving Uncle Sam. His pay might seem good in the UK but was a miserly amount by American standards. She seemed to be in love with several Americans at the same time, probably working on a permutation, to ensure success. She worked at nights for a time for Radio Cabs but they had to let her go, as the saying goes, when the phone bills came home to roost. One of her paramours had gone home to the US and she spent the long night hours talking to him at the cab company's expense. Incoming calls for taxis were ignored and potential passengers went to rival establishments. She was a disaster as an employee, although she did make the office look pretty. Her carelessness with other people's money did not make her any less attractive.

I had seen her from time to time in the Rutland Hotel bar, which was base camp for some of the better-dressed cabbies. I didn't really know her, but we had exchanged the odd word from time to time. I had been sheltering in the bar one evening, reluctant to go to work because of the atrocious weather conditions, which were a fatal combination of high winds and torrential rain. It was a night for staying by the fireside at home or sitting snug in a pub with friends. The trains were running late and business was dead. It was a wild night of gusting winds and rain, and although I had experienced worse, it was bad enough to drive others off the road. Jo-Jo was with a tall, taciturn man who did not seem able to smile. That at least was my opinion, formed from his stony facial expression, and this was strange, because where Jo-Jo was there were usually high spirits and laughter. I decided that it was probably her latest boyfriend, jealously guarding her from imagined threats to their relationship. A wiser man would have appreciated that being interested in her, but also interesting in his own right, he would be much surer of her loyalty. That would only apply if the word 'loyal' was part of Jo-Jo's lexicon, of course. To my surprise she approached me with a smile and a request. I don't think anyone ever said no to Jo-Jo.

'Have you got your taxi outside? If you have we'd like you to take us to the Dean Village.' Work that dropped into one's lap could not be ignored, so, despite the dreadful weather, off we went. The longest way, via Queensferry Road, would be the quickest, but drivers are always being accused of profiteering, so it was the direct route for us. This was an extremely hazardous journey on a night like this. The cab was being buffeted about and I had to concentrate hard to get us down to the village safely because strong gusts of wind hitting the open side of the cab rocked the whole vehicle alarmingly. At times it could be pushed suddenly to one side by as much as a yard. Apart from the odd glance, I had no opportunity to use my little safety mirrors, because total concentration was required to avoid an accident. Jo-Jo and her paramour were locked in a passionate embrace, and as far as I could tell, quite oblivious to the dangerous weather conditions. All my attention was required to negotiate the twists and turns met in reaching the Dean Village.

When we arrived in the village the sliding glass partition was opened and Jo-Jo's voice announced: 'Change of plan, driver; sorry, but back to the West End. He's left his gloves in the hotel.' This was fine by me, and much better, because I would be paid for both legs of the journey.

When we got back to the door of the hotel I was paid off with a minimal tip, and Jo-Jo went back into the hotel, while her boyfriend, without recovering his gloves, headed towards the Caledonian Hotel entrance. The miserable sod was probably going to catch a bus somewhere, depriving me of further business. I was undecided on what to do next, but I was out in the rain now and thought that I would look for some work. A busy train must have recently arrived at the Caledonian Station because taxis were streaming out of the side entrance like contestants in a miniature road race. I was not going to miss out, so I swept into the station, where a long queue of prospective passengers was waiting in line and I was the only cab in the place.

As I drew up at the head of the queue I did my usual glancing check of the cab's interior. It was then that I saw it, and was shocked. It was a horrible sight: a very recently used rubber item (the word 'condom' was not in common usage then), lying on the floor of the cabin. I dived out of the driver's door and shoved aside a passenger who was about to open the rear door for himself. Pushing my way inside I leaned forward and opened the offside door, simultaneously kicking the offensive object out of the cab. The whole action took but a second or two, and as I backed out I held the door open for my puzzled passengers. As fast as I could make it, we were off.

Twenty minutes later I was back in a short queue of cabs ready to pick up the stragglers still waiting for taxis. The continental billet-doux still lay in solitary state, in the middle of the circus round which the taxis approached their fares, but typically no one could see it, apparently. Station staff stepped carefully over it and cabs skirted round it. Taxi drivers talked among themselves about it, all curious as to how it could possibly have been deposited there; it was a real mystery. Passengers in the taxi queue were preoccupied with the roof structures of the station. A few pigeons had a peck at it, but it was evidently not to their taste, and it lay there for hours.

We are all supposed to love lovers, but I would certainly have some seriously hateful words with Jo-Jo when next I met her.

26

THE FIREWID KING

The Top End rank at the top of Leith Walk was not one of my favourite ranks, but it was 9.30 at night, and only two other taxis were lined up on it, so I became number three. It could be a very educational spot. The nightly skirmishing, an inevitable feature of the area, had hardly begun and would liven up when the pubs closed at ten o'clock. Things were looking promising, with several deadbeats and half-drunks eyeing up the available talent. TV sports broadcasting had not yet got a grip on the minds of the populace, and this was much better anyway because it was the real thing. By a few minutes after ten a throng of rubbernecking spectators, a few hundred strong, would be on hand and ready to enjoy the free spectator sport invariably on offer.

It was like the days of ancient Rome. First into the arena would be drunks versus drunks. The second spectacle would be police versus drunks. The third item, one of the most enjoyable, was watching the women, whose male friends had been taken away in a black Maria, attacking the police. The grand finale would be gallant but misguided semi-drunk men whose aim was to earn Brownie points and perhaps something better by defending the slags against the brutal police. The strange thing was that the outcome was always the same. The police always won.

If the arrested persons went quietly, they would be quickly transferred to the cells in the High Street. If they were silly enough to throw caution to the wind and actually draw blood from the veins of an officer of the law then the journey to the High Street took considerably longer, as the van toured the highways and byways of the city, always taking the longest way round. During the journey the van would rock and roll its way to the Bridewell. Pedestrians along the way would be aware of muffled shouts and the odd crash, bang and wallop as the van drove past them. It was not unusual for the van to be required to make a pick-up from the police box at the Top End every fifteen minutes on a busy night, because a police box is fairly small. The strange thing was that the regulars took this mayhem to be the status quo, and business went on in and around the site without interruption.

The Deep Sea chip shop was doing its usual roaring trade, providing quality merchandise to a stream of demanding customers. This was in stark contrast to the row of bedraggled ladies of pleasure on the pavement patrol who looked capable of providing anything but that. I was stuck on the rank, knowing that no movement would be likely for some time. I had seen it a hundred times before, and although the cast changed, the play was essentially the same. When things died down business would start for us once more. I was completely relaxed watching the almost choreographed moves when I became aware of the overpowering stench of hot fat, fried fish, chips and vinegar. At the same moment a soft, shy voice addressed me and I knew instinctively that it could only be Tommy. He was his usual picture of sartorial elegance. Bib and brace overalls, dungaree jacket, flat cap square on his head and wellies with the tops turned down in a raffish off-duty manner. Under his arm was a gigantic newspaper-wrapped parcel from which steam clouds were drifting skywards. His opening sally was typical of him, and completely logical.

'Ah kent it was you as soon as I seen you, Mr Finnally.' Having nothing better to do I was, in truth, quite pleased to see him. The last time we had spoken was when I had called at his home, so I enquired after the health of his nearest and dearest.

'They're great, every'hings great.' His chest visibly swelled with pride as he announced, 'You should see the wee fella noo; he's a wee bugger, so he is. Intae every'hing if ye don't watch him, so he is. He's a right wee bugger, so he is, an' that's a true fact.' I agreed with Tommy that his news was indeed 'great' and thought it wise to avoid the subject of wee Tommy's musical prodigality in case his hilarity made him drop his parcel. Instead I enquired after his lady wife. 'She's great an' aw. She's got a wee night job noo. So every'hing's great.'

An unworthy thought flashed through my mind as I wondered if she was providing competition for the ranks of the girls lined up outside the Deep Sea. If she was, then her earnings were likely to be affected by her chronic shyness. I dismissed the thought as unkind and pressed for details. 'Och well,' confessed Tommy, 'it's no much o' a job. It's just washin' up in a café, but Ah hiv tae get ma ain tea, ken.' In typical Tommy style he raised his arm to indicate the steaming bundle in case I was in any doubt about the veracity of his statement. In case I had not noticed, he explained, 'That's what this is, fish an' chips for me an' the wee fella.'

I hinted to Tommy that his supper would be getting cold, but he was in no hurry to move on. We discussed the advantages and drawbacks of a working wife and how valuable any extra income was during the present hard times. It was clear that Tommy had something to tell me, but his ability in the small talk world was limited. After a few more minutes he came out with it.

'Did Ah tell ye that Ah wiz on the superann' noo, Mr Finnally? Aye, Ah've got a job for life, noo that Ah'm pernament wi' the corpy an' a pension at the end o' it forbye; what do ye think o' that?' I was genuinely delighted for him. No one worked harder at keeping the streets clean, and for twelve years or more he had been messed about by being classified as a temporary employee of the council. He would now have a regular site and this would draw attention to just how thorough he was in his work. I was tickled pink for him. He suddenly added, in a remarkable shaft of perception: 'Do you no wish you was on the superann', Mr Finnally?' It was game, set and match to Tommy, because he had me there.

In a rearguard action I explained that a pension was something that I had given serious consideration to and that any day now I would be approaching an insurance company to take out a pension policy to take care of my old age. I also added that I was now probably unemployable, having become used to the freedom of self-employment, when in reality every customer becomes your boss. I told him that I would like to stay that way. It was then that Tommy dropped his bombshell.

'Ah bet you didnae ken that Ah had ma ain business at one time, Mr Finnally? Aye.' At this point, seeing incredulity in my face, he paused before stressing, 'Ah wiz a very successful businessman an' aw, an' that's a true fact.' I was intrigued. His supper could freeze as far as I was concerned, because I wanted to know more about this unlikely scenario. As a captive audience I was in the front row of the stalls and Tommy expanded on his former business career. It was quite a story.

'Aye,' he began, 'Ah had ma ain business aw right. Ah wiz in the big time an' that's a true fact. Business wiz great, really great. Ah had a big yaird doon Canonmills when they wiz poolin' doon the hooses. Ah had six blokes working fur me full-time and as mony again was working part-time. Ah wiz doin' OK.' Tommy's eyes misted over as he recalled those far-off days. 'Ah made a lot o' money, Mr Finnally, Ah kin tell ye, Ah made a lot o' money. Mind, Ah wiz an awffy man fur the drink in them days.' He smiled at the memory and continued. 'Ah wiz never sober.' A sheepish but boastful grin came over his face as he said this. He was clearly proud of his former capacity for drink.

'So you drank yourself out of the business, did you, Tommy?' It was an obvious conclusion and my question was delivered in a sympathetic way, but my self-interest, as usual, had jumped to the forefront of my mind. If Tommy had been able to create a successful business, what might I do when I extracted the details from the gullible Tommy? 'Tell me more about your business, Tommy,' I coaxed.

Tommy needed no encouragement to continue his narrative. 'Naw, naw it wiznae the drink,' he softly protested, clearly still back in time. 'It wiz sheer bad luck, and Ah got done as well.' My prospects were looking brighter by the minute. Having picked his brains for the idea I could probably convert it to millions. An insurance policy could cover the eventuality of bad luck, and as for being 'done', the culprit would have to rise very early in the morning to do that to me. I was confident of success, and asked him what kind of business he had been in.

'Did Ah no' tell ye, Mr Finnally?' He looked surprised. 'Ah wiz in the firewid trade. They cried me the Firewid King, aye, that's who Ah wiz, Ah wiz the Firewid King, an' that's a true fact. It wiz no' lang efter the war or a bit later than that I suppose. I'm no really sure when it wiz, for it wiz a long time ago, ken.' My hopes were dashed. Firewood was a thing of the past and new smokeless zones were being introduced. Tommy prattled on. 'Me an' the boys used to start early in the mornins and get stuck in, so that we could finish at dinner-time an' go tae the pub. Never came oot until closin' time, and we wid take a cairry-oot back tae the yaird and get smashed. Ah wiz buying drinks fur them aw. Ah wiz a right bampot. Ma old lady always said Ah wiz a edjit. Ah wiz stayin' wi' her then 'cause Ah wisnae merrit.' The dream had gone now, since he might as well be telling me how a fortune could be made in recycling acetylene lamps making gas mantles. I still might learn something when he told me how he had failed though.

'It wiz a cash business, nae cheques nor nuthin' an' Ah never had no time fur banks an' that. So Ah goes up tae George Street tae Grays the Ironmongers; they had the best name in the toon fur their stuff, an' Ah says tae the boy behind the coonter. "Gi'es yer very bestest and strongest fireproof cash box in the place, money nae object." An' the boy sells me yin aboot this size.'

Tommy demonstrated with his free hand a box about twelve inches by six. It was a bit like a one-armed fisherman illustrating the length of his catch or the one that got away. 'It cost me a shillin' or two, Ah kin tell ye. But it wiz the best. Ye see Ah wiz right fly. It had tae be fireproof because Ah used tae plank it in the firewid at night and when Ah went oot an' that. See everybody Ah met used tae tap me fur a few bob when they kent Ah had the readies on me. Naebody kent where it was stashed away except me, so it wiz quite safe.' I had a sinking feeling in my stomach that it would not require the services of a Maigret or a Hercule Poirot to work out where the money went. It would not have taken his loyal employees long to discover where Tommy, in his drunken state, had hidden his loot. I put this to him, but he brushed aside any suggestion that any of his boys could have been implicated. My doubt must have shown clearly in my face because he spelled out the sequence of events slowly and clearly, as if speaking to a child:

'It wiz like this, Mr Finnally. Ah had had a right skinfy an Ah wiz sleepin' it aff in ma scratcher, deed tae the world, when Ah hears ma old lady shoutin' at me. It wiz aboot three o'clock in the mornin', ken.' Tommy's face reflected some of the outrage that he must have felt that fateful day when dragged from his slumber to reality. 'She wakes me up an' she says tae me, "Tommy Souness," she says, "whit have you been up tae? There's twa big polis at the door wantin' ye." "Nu'hing, Ma," Ah says, "Ah've never done nu'hing."'

I had never seen Tommy so animated. He was reliving what must have been a major trauma in his life.

'Tae tell you the truth, Mr Finnally, Ah didnae ken what Ah had done the night before, I wiz that blotto. Anyway, Ah gets up and goes tae the door, an' right enough there's them big bobbies standin' on the step. So Ah says, "Whit can Ah dae for youse?" Bein' fly. Gie'in' nu'hing away like. "Are you Mr Souness?" one o' them says. "Mr Thomas Souness?" "Aye," Ah says, "that's me." Then the ither yin says. "The Mr Thomas Souness that used tae

hae a timber yard doon Canonmills?" Ah put him right. "Aye,"
Ah says, "that's me, but you've got it wrang." Ah had ma wits
aboot me even in the middle o' the night, blootered as a wiz. Ah
says, "Ah *am* the Thomas Souter that *hiz* a timber yaird doon
the Canonmills. They cry me the Firewid King!" "Well, your
Majesty," says the cheeky bugger, "you've just got abdicated
'cause it's brunt down." An' it had, Mr Finnally; just like the
polis said, it had brunt doon.'

During his telling of the tale Tommy had displayed a remarkable gift for mimicry and was able to imitate his mother's voice
and that of the two policemen, even getting the grammar
and pronunciation right. Now his voice faltered and a pained
expression settled on his face. Even the passage of years had not
dimmed the pain of the loss of his business premises and stock.
'Ah didnae ken aboot insurance an' that.' He confessed.

'At least your money would be safe, Tommy. The fireproof
safety box would have seen to that.' I was almost pleading with
him to confirm that it had not been stolen.

'Ah only wish you wiz right, Mr Finnally, Ah only wish you
wiz right, an' that's a true fact. Ah had over five hunner' quid in
that box, but like Ah telt ye, Ah wiz done.'

'You mean the money was stolen, Tommy?' It confirmed my
hunch; I had been right from the beginning.

'Naw, Mr Finnally, it wisnae stole, but Ah wiz robbed just
the same.' He said this dismissively, irritated by my inability to
grasp the simple facts of the incident. I opened my mouth to ask
for an explanation of what to me was a complete contradiction.
If the money was gone it was stolen, and he had been well and
truly done. He read my mind.

'It couldnae get stole, Ah've telt ye that, Ah wiz the only one
who kent where it wiz.' His faith in the honesty of his employees
was touching. 'Ah got done aw right, Mr Finnally. It's hard tae
believe it but the fire was that hot that it brunt the box, the
money an' every'hing. Nu'hing wiz left. The polis an' the fire
brigade an' me searched everywhere. Oh aye, Ah got done aw

right. It wiz they buggers in George Street what done me. They selt me a duff box an' that's a true fact.'

Tommy was a trusting soul despite a lifetime of having the sugar taken out of his tea by a string of shady operators.

27

McPHEE OF THAT ILK

It is not every day that you meet a real, live, walking, talking idiot, and it took a minute or three before the penny dropped. I should have realised this the moment he introduced himself.

'I'm Hector Hamish McPhee of that Ilk, and first in line to the Chieftainship of that Clan.' His claim defied comment, and his confidence was total. He was instantly christened He-Haw, conjoining his Hector Hamish in an easy-to-remember linkage. The layabouts and hangers-on who habitually spent their days and nights in the various coffee houses and cafés in the Forrest Road area of the city, thought that He-Haw was heaven-sent. He had a spending habit and a seemingly unlimited supply of white five-pound notes, and he had fortuitously discovered a group of instant friends.

In De Marco's café, the most popular rendezvous in the area and not the most expensive, the genial proprietor was always tolerant of his hard-up clientele. There was always something going on and the place always looked busy. This activity attracted paying customers, and surprisingly enough the food was excellent. His chicken Maryland had to be experienced to be believed: it was a culinary delight with fried banana, lots of breaded chicken pieces, a homemade tomato sauce and a double portion of potato chips. A single pineapple ring on top gave the dish a festive air whatever the season. I used to call in and order it regularly, as it was my favourite dish, and as a result of my frequent visits I was considered to be one of the 'in' crowd.

I never picked up a fare there, but Forrest Road was a busy area and never far out of my way.

What brought McPhee of that Ilk into the café will never be known, but the habitués instantly recognised that they had a 'live one' here, as the saying goes. He was instantly popular, and as an apparently lonely individual, he appreciated his new friends and considered it his duty to treat them to coffee. He naturally enough wore a kilt at all times, in a tartan that he insisted was exclusive to the heir to the clan chieftainship. His sporran was the real attraction, as it was permanently stuffed with the aforementioned large white fivers. His willingness to spend them ensured a warm welcome whenever he chose to appear, which was very often over a fairly short period of time.

Where he came from was one of life's mysteries, as was where he went eventually. He was a figure of fun, but everyone had the good sense not to laugh at him, at least when he was around. He was thought to be in his early twenties, but this opinion was based on things that he said and referred to from time to time, while others were equally convinced that he was not yet twenty. There were great gaps in his knowledge, particularly about human nature, but he seemed to be well read. With his kilt he wore a hairy tweed jacket, heavy woollen stockings and brogues. This was fair enough, but he spoiled it by wearing a huge Tam o' Shanter and carrying an ornate walking stick. His head was small and his hat was large. He was extremely tall at six feet five inches-plus, and anorexic thin. At first glance he looked like a giant stick insect in a kilt and a flat cap, and sporting hairy legs. Stick insect or not, he had that well-stuffed sporran! He thought he was Jack the Lad, or perhaps Larry the Laird, but it was universally acknowledged that he was a prize eejit, as we say in these parts. This opinion was never expressed to his face, you will understand, but regularly mentioned behind his back. Hector Hamish McPhee of that Ilk was far too free with his money for any such thing, and he allowed no one to pay for their own coffee if he was about. This was not as good for trade as might be thought, because the regulars held off from buying, in case the McPhee happened along.

He was, he claimed, a keen collector of walking sticks and was never seen without one. A few of the less indolent of the café's clients made a beeline for the 'Lane Sales' in Thistle Street, where a bin of assorted and unwanted walking sticks could be picked up for a few pence. These were gradually and individually released, with impressive stories about their provenance. They would be offered for sale to the impressionable McPhee, who would snap them up, paying the asking price with enthusiasm. In fact, at one stage there were so many genuine Harry Lauder curly walking sticks littered about the café that the genial proprietor lost his geniality and became quite cross. He insisted that they be removed in case a paying customer fell over one of them and broke a leg. He-Haw would buy anything in the stick line so long as it had an historical connection, real or imagined, and would pay the ever-rising asking prices without demur. His luck had been in when he had stumbled upon this particular café, because in a very short space of time he had acquired a treasure trove of walking sticks. Two crooks, one formerly the property of a John Brown and the other of a Queen Victoria, were fortuitously unearthed in different parts of the city on the same day. How lucky can you get? Sir Walter Scott, Robert Burns and even Field-Marshal Haig were all waiting in the wings, or at least their former properties were. Engraved initial bands freely added and altered at will were helpful in authenticating the former owners. All good things come to an end, and suddenly He-Haw lost interest in sticks. A cottage industry failed overnight and many fires were lit with priceless relics.

You do not keep a good man down for long though, and Hector Hamish McPhee of that Ilk now developed a new and much more exciting and expensive passion: cars. He was a true-to-life Toad of Toad Hall in this respect. Not just any old cars, but exotic ones; if they were not unusual they were of no interest to the McPhee. Where he was getting his fivers from became a matter of debate. He couldn't be a bank robber, because even a sketchy description would have given him away. His first purchase was a dream, in the form of an exquisite low chassis numbered pre-war BMW roadster. His next was a genuine GI Jeep, whose stencilled bonnet number exactly matched the one shown in a wartime issue of *Picture Post*, and according to the story in the magazine it was the personal transport of General Patton. It was, Hector Hamish assured us, the one he was in when killed in the crash, though the vehicle showed no signs of repairs having been carried out on it. How lucky can you get, take two.

The one snag in the creating of this collection was that he could not drive.

About this time someone revealed to him that I was a professional driver; although not the more accurate description of lowly taxi driver, it was a version of the truth. He-Haw immediately surmised that I drove for Ecurie Ecosse or some such outfit, and I became his target. His next find was a Singer Le Mans 'Flying fixed head coupé'. This was the weirdest car that I have ever driven in my life, as it was so low-slung that without the roof open to allow one's head to poke out, a normal-sized person could not see through the windscreen. A person of challenged growth would have no trouble with forward vision but would not be able to reach the pedals, so it had limited appeal. It ran very well, but as soon as the rain came on, as it regularly does throughout the year in Scotland, it was necessary to pull to the side of the road and crouch down under the closed roof to sit out the storm. It was a tad impractical, but undaunted, our Mr Toad pressed on in assembling his collection. A Ford V8 Pilot was the most sensible. A rare Lea Francis and a 'bull-nosed' Morris Cowley came next. The white fiver tree must have been blossoming because within days a Lincoln Continental arrived, followed by a Bristol, and even a 'Baby' Austin. Finally he found from somewhere a truly magnificent Auburn.

A storage garage of some sort had to be found, because as the fleet of exotic machinery grew, the available places to park the collection reduced. When the McPhee was not dreaming of his Highland mansion, he lived in a fairly modest flat in a tenement building in Marchmont, and for some inexplicable reason the architects of the 1880s had not considered garages to be of importance. This would have been an insurmountable problem to a normal person, but the Lanky Laird took it in his stride. Ordering me to leave his cars in quiet residential areas outside suitably grand detached houses solved the parking problem. Some of the other, less exotic cars were left in public or private car parks. It takes at least two people to distribute cars all over the place, and it soon became clear that many of the volunteer drivers had as much ability in this sphere as the McPhee himself, and dents and scratches soon appeared on the priceless collection. I had been appointed as his official, unpaid, professional driver and my advice was taken as gospel about any matters automotive. Yet He-Haw had difficulty grasping the concept of a garage. He may have had other reasons, because someone would have to sign the lease and negotiate with the utility companies. The bold McPhee also became quite stroppy with my frequent disappearances when I was away earning a living in my taxi. He felt that it was an honour to drive him about since he was, after all, heir to the etc., etc.

Eventually the dream came true. Someone signed the necessary documents and reality arrived. That there were no workshops was a minor matter. Mechanics? We would see to that anon. I was not very happy at being included as half of the 'we'. It is hard to keep a low profile when driving an open Auburn roadster. With the dickey seat open and four or five student types hanging out of it and yelling at any girls they spotted, it was difficult to be anonymous. The crowd in the front were not so ostentatious, since the seating was low and the doors high. I also discovered that He-Haw and insurance were strangers to each other, and road tax even less acceptable to him than it was to Jock of Jock's Taxi Co. fame. The aim was to become purveyors of classic automobiles to the gentry, who are a dying breed if they ever existed. The basic trouble was twofold. One was that when He-Haw bought a car he couldn't bear to part with it, and the second was that he knew less than nothing about business. That he knew nothing about cars we can take as already understood.

You cannot keep secret the fact that a prize idiot is on the loose and that his pockets are bulging with the folding stuff. Dealers turned up at this young entrepreneur's new business premises, and instead of offering to buy from him, they would sell him anything at all. This often included the vehicle that they had arrived in. It is no hardship to have to take a bus home, especially if your pockets are stuffed with twice the value of the motor car that you have just offloaded to an ass. He-Haw was even more stupid in his car dealing than he had been when running his walking-stick business. The unit value did not seem to matter at all, and a glib-tongued dealer would congratulate Hector Hamish McPhee on his astuteness in spotting a niche in the market, whilst offloading some unroadworthy heap before disappearing into the sunset clutching his profits. He-Haw did not know how to haggle, or even how to say no, or how to value a motorcar. He knew as much about the trade magazines and value booklets as he did about flying saucers. Had he been heir to the Bank of England, his business would have failed.

He even bought cars without title, and I would one day become involved in one such case and would risk my life over He-Haw's stupidity.

28

THE DIAGNOSTIC DOG

PC Bert, despite his ambitions about joining the CID, had settled for helping to establish the fledgling dog section being set up in Edinburgh. The unit had very few vehicles, which meant that a handler, at the end of his shift, had to pick up the next shift handler before being dropped off at home. A plus for the dog handlers was that they were always attending scenes of crime and had a very high arrest rate to their credit. Although Bert was making his mark in the new dog section, he must still have harboured thoughts of the CID, because he asked me to meet him at the end of his shift before going on to have a hush-hush meeting with a CID sergeant. As in most jobs it is often who you know that counts, and for Bert to arrange a meeting relating to police business in his own time meant that something important had to be discussed. An added incentive to my going along was his remark that the meeting would take place at a party being hosted by a doctor with a passion for pipe music where, he assured me, I would be most welcome.

The venue was a ground-floor flat overlooking The Meadows, at Tollcross, just round the corner from the doctor's consulting rooms. I think there was a connecting passage between the two parts of his premises, but I could not be sure on that point. We were welcomed by the good doctor, who was surprisingly light skinned for someone who claimed to hail from the Khyber Pass. Perhaps among his forebears there might have been some member of a Highland regiment who had been posted to that

God-forsaken part of the world. He certainly knew his stuff with regard to pipe music and showed us proof copies of his soon-to-be-published book on the subject. This was not just any run-of-the-mill book but one that today must be a collector's item. Somehow Dr Soros had persuaded the various world champion exponents of all types of bagpipe music to allow their skills to be recorded, and a tape of their performances was packaged within the cover of the book. Whilst a chapter of the book would describe the origins of say, a dirge, a section of it would be devoted to the most famous ones and the story of their creation, together with the sheet music. The doctor must have had a touch of genius about him because he had advance orders, at an eye-watering price, from all over the world.

Naturally, when we arrived the recording from the book was playing at maximum volume for the benefit of those attending the party. Non-attendees could also enjoy the festivities because a few windows had been left open.

Bert's CID man was not present, so we consoled ourselves by enjoying the hospitality laid on by the good doctor. Whisky was the only drink available, and it was doled out in liberal quantities. I was not a whisky drinker and mingled with the four or five ladies present. There could be no mistake they were indeed ladies. I chatted to them and discovered a schoolteacher, a civil servant and a lady solicitor – it was quite unusual to find a lady at the Bar at that time. However, it was difficult to hold a conversation because of the accompanying racket – my personal view is that, much as I love the sound of bagpipes, I prefer them to be played at a distance. Close to they hurt the eardrums. When the cassette player was switched off the good doctor demonstrated some intricate fingering on a chanter.

The room where all this was happening was a front lounge and the curtains were wide open, throwing light across the street outside and onto the adjacent Meadows. The houses were stone-built but the sound in the street outside must have been deafening. It was after eleven o'clock at night and no one seemed to care about complaints from neighbours.

Suddenly a door into the lounge was opened and a naked male figure entered the room. Evidently there was another party going on too. To say he was naked is a slight exaggeration, since he was in fact wearing his socks, a wrist watch and an extremely smug expression. I was the only person present to show any surprise. The lady lawyer, the school-ma'am and the civil servant simply chatted on. The CID officer – for that is who he was – apologised for disturbing us but stated that he had left his cigarettes and lighter on the mantelpiece above the fire. He picked them up and turned to retreat, when he spotted Bert.

'I need a word with you, so don't leave until we get the chance of a chat,' he informed him, and then spoke briefly to the ladies quite unconcernedly, and no one took a blind bit of notice. There was no pointing or sniggering or even a remark passed. It was taken as completely normal behaviour. He then announced, 'Must dash, don't want the lady to get cold.' With that he nonchalantly strolled from the room. The surprising thing to me was the reaction of those in the room. It was like the Emperor's new clothes; was I the only one who could not see them?

More people drifted in and the good doctor broke off from the serious business of bagpipes to pay some attention to his guests. 'We're getting a bit short of women,' he observed. 'I'll round up a few.' He opened a drawer and produced an address book and started to telephone some of the numbers listed there. It was now after midnight and I could hear one side of the conversations.

'Rik Soros here. So you're in bed! Get up and come round. I know it's late but I need you here. Grab a cab and get round here right away.' Strangely, for a man from the Khyber Pass, he had a public school accent. It sounded more like orders than invitations and sure enough within half an hour half a dozen fresh faces had joined us. There was a bit of moaning from the new arrivals, not to the good doctor, but to us, their fellow guests.

'I've got school at eight-thirty tomorrow,' said one, and I couldn't help noticing that she wore a wedding band. 'And I've not finished marking my class papers and it has to be done by the morning.' Her husband must have been an understanding man. Others muttered too, and I thought that he must have been something of a Svengali to wield such power.

Most coloured doctors that I had come across refused to drink alcohol on religious grounds, but this one drank more than his share of the MacStagger, and as the alcohol made him more talkative I began to find out more about him. His wife, a Scottish girl, had left him, taking the kids with her, and he was slightly off the rails.

I asked him about the ease with which he managed to induce such charming company from their beds to attend what was clearly not an uncommon event. The good doctor explained that it had all come about since his wife had gone. 'It's all the work of my diagnostic dog,' the doctor declared, introducing me to a mutt that seemed a nice enough animal – one of those excessively hairy creatures who peer at you through a tangle of facial hair. It sniffed a lot.

'It can tell if a woman is randy and game for it or not. Look at that lot.' He indicated his lady guests. 'You'd think that butter wouldn't melt in their mouths, but there's no randier bunch in the city.' I wondered if his dog was for sale, but said nothing.

He had been told that I drove a taxi, and was keen for me to call a couple of days later, as he had arranged to go to Hawick to see his wife and children and wanted company. We would use his drop-head Austin Atlantic, a model that I would enjoy driving, and he would naturally supply the petrol.

As it got later people emerged from the other party – music lovers and lovers who were tone deaf. The host of party number two was a senior lecturer at a local veterinary college, whose large drink-induced strawberry nose spoiled his former handsome looks. Despite the number of ladies apparently available, all I took home from the party was Bert and an instructive book,

Forensic Medicine, which the doctor lent me after we had got chatting on the subject.

Having finalised the arrangements for the trip to meet Dr Soros' wife I went back on duty for the rest of the night with lots to think about. Edinburgh was relatively small, but all human life was here if you knew where to look.

When I turned up to carry out my driving duties for Dr Soros, it was to find that he had either forgotten the appointment or was too busy to attend. I hung around as desperate people do. Twenty minutes later he appeared, driving his Austin Atlantic roadster, and in fairness he greeted me like a long-lost cousin as he invited me to sit in the passenger's seat. The diagnostic dog lay on the back seat, under the tonneau cover, and we were off. Our journey from Tollcross to Mayfield, if not a world record, should certainly have appeared in the *Guinness Book of Records*, if such a record had been in existence. Under the sun visor he had a notice affixed which stated 'Doctor on call – Police Surgeon'. The good doctor clearly interpreted this as a licence to travel at any speed he considered appropriate.

We screeched to a halt outside a fashionable bar restaurant, and Dr Soros led us (me and the diagnostic dog) inside, where he was greeted warmly by the lady behind the bar. The dog's reaction instantly pointed her out as someone likely to enjoy one of Dr Soros' soirées, and I made a careful note. Soros accepted a free brandy, a lager and lime for me, but nothing at all for the pooch. Driving on, we stopped and started a dozen times before we cleared the city limits. The good doctor, having consumed at least eight large brandies, was no longer fit to drive and I took over the wheel.

Although now in control of the car, I was not completely in charge, since I was instructed to stop several more times during the journey. During these breaks the dog identified seven ladies worthy of further consideration and I, being on duty as it were, and having had only two lagers and lime, was therefore up to the task of recording the various locations.

The routine was always the same. We would be warmly welcomed, the doctor would accept a drink and I would refuse one, and our diagnostic dog either did or didn't point. It was quite amazing to study the wide range of ladies that the dog picked out – from the young and pretty to the old and matronly. I clearly had a lot to learn about women.

It was well after two o'clock when we arrived at the house where the estranged Mrs Soros was billeted. We entered the gate into the garden and up a path that led to a side door. When Mrs Soros appeared she had clearly been waiting for us for some time and she was one very angry female. Undoubtedly very attractive and pretty in normal circumstances, her face was now contorted with rage as she screamed at him.

'One o'clock for lunch!' she yelled. 'We'll talk over our problems and discuss our future together you said, and you arrive here drunk!' Soros looked at me for support and I admired the garden. One thing that Bert had taught me was never to interfere between a husband and a wife, as it was always a no-win situation. I was not to get off so easily, though, and the wife drew me into the picture. 'And what have you brought him for, moral support, I suppose? Well, you're out of luck.' I thought I might pour oil on those troubled waters but found that words failed me, so I indicated by hand signals that I was only the driver. I suppose I looked like the village idiot on the loose.

Mrs Soros turned on the doctor again. 'And the kids, they've been excited all morning because their daddy was coming to see them. Look at them!' I had not noticed the two children hovering in the doorway. Two milk-coffee-coloured little boys were shyly peeping out and clearly disturbed by the upsetting behaviour of their mother. Soros turned to me and made what seemed to me a very wise decision. 'I think we should leave, as we are clearly not welcome here.' It was the understatement of the year.

As we turned back down the garden path Mrs Soros continued her tirade. I climbed in behind the wheel and Soros slumped in the passenger seat. It was then that I remembered the dog and looked around for it. It had never moved from under its cover, and all I could see were two gloomy eyes looking fearfully out from between its two front paws. As a result I never found what his diagnosis of Mrs Soros would have been. But never mind; it was unlikely that I would ever be back in the Hawick area, though in taxi driving you never really know where you might end up.

Unlike our outward journey, we travelled non-stop back to Tollcross. Soros slept throughout and only awoke when we arrived at the surgery door. He looked at his watch and confirmed that I had done a good job, as he was just in time for his late afternoon surgery. He still looked drunk to me but was quite confident that he could cope with a room full of patients. He never offered me any payment for the trip to Hawick and I never asked for any, but he did solemnly advise me that if ever I had the misfortune to fall into the hands of the police for a drink-related driving offence I was to be sure to send for him. He would see to it and all would be well. He invited me into his surgery for a 'quick one', and as I drank my lager his clients were kept waiting while he listened to telephone messages on a machine I had never seen before. The wonders of technology never cease to amaze – perhaps someday he would be able to consult his patients without the drag of actually having to examine them.

The national press ignored it, and according to our local newspapers the item was of very little interest, and so the news was hidden away in the middle pages. An Edinburgh doctor had been struck off by the General Medical Council. There was no reason given. The name of the former doctor was given as R. Soros. Those in the know began to talk, and his secret was soon out and into the public domain. His diagnostic dog turned out to be a smoke screen: the real answer was his little black book. His sideline had been abortions for the famous, the well connected and the well-heeled. Blackmail is an ugly word, but even some senior police officers' wives, girlfriends and secretaries had been obliged to him, as had Edinburgh's café society at large. The police investigations were carried out with little enthusiasm, due no doubt to the number of investigating officers who were beholden to the good doctor, but clearly he had to be brought to book.

It was generally agreed that he was a splendid chap and all that, but no longer competent. At an early stage of the enquiries he had clearly been tipped off that the heat was on, and his nerve went completely, but, such was the demand for his services that he continued his abortion facility. Luckily or unluckily, depending on your point of view, he had a friend who was not only completely fearless, but also of dubious moral integrity. When Dr Soros had been reduced to a gibbering wreck, he issued instructions to his pal on which end of the knitting needle to insert, and it was business as usual for a time. Unfortunately for all concerned, some of the women who underwent these amateurish procedures were obliged to turn to their local hospitals for remedial action. VIPs they might be, but once admitted to hospital they became simply patients, and as surgeons and doctors are not all dimwits it rapidly became clear that there was an incompetent at large who was a menace to women. As the net tightened many of Soros' former friends and clients deserted him and sold him down the river.

About this time there was a demand that abortions should be legalised, subject to strict controls, and the pressure was such that our politicians, knowing a vote winner when they see one, soon passed the necessary laws. By a strange coincidence, within a few months Mr Soros became Dr Soros again, when his name was restored to the register of the General Medical Council. He did not return to Edinburgh to practise. He should now be long retired, so it is quite safe to visit your GP, even if he hails from foreign parts, is very well spoken and sometimes plays the bagpipes.

He might even have a strange-looking dog.

29

MONTY'S MOTOR

From the moment that I slid behind the huge steering wheel, and looked along the miles of bonnet to the flagless pennant rod, I knew that I was going to buy it. The car was a true limousine, long and black, with a division between the front and rear compartments, which were spacious and inviting. The ritzy interior was finished in light tan hide, so it was a bit like a taxi, but *posh*! The rear seat was as big and luxurious as a sofa and the occasional seats, which stowed away in the dividing partition, provided forward-facing seating for another two passengers, or three at a push. These extra seats were wide and comfortable enough for the longest journeys. In emergencies the car could seat nine, including the driver, and would quickly transport me to tycoonery.

I was smitten, and through my rose-coloured spectacles the car was perfect, but could I afford it? Business had been getting better, or perhaps I had been getting better at the business. By doubling the size of my fleet to two cars I reckoned that I could double my income, and for some weeks I had been on the look-out for another taxi plate, but they were as scarce as hen's teeth and impossibly expensive to buy. Then I saw the advertisement, boxed in an eye-catching heavy black line, and it called out to me. It intrigued me, and as I feel sure that sometimes fate plays a hand, I was convinced that someone somewhere had willed me to notice the opportunity.

GENERAL MONTGOMERY'S PERSONAL
STAFF CAR. CHAUFFEUR-DRIVEN AND
MAINTAINED REGARDLESS OF EXPENSE.
SURPLUS TO REQUIREMENTS OF
LEADING PUBLIC COMPANY. SUIT LUXURY
LIMOUSINE OR PRIVATE HIRE OPERATIVE.
NEEDS MINOR ATTENTION. PHONE WAV
2020. PRINCIPALS ONLY NEED APPLY.

This was just what I had been looking for to exploit the lucrative weekend wedding market. Three or four weddings each weekend would bring in a tidy sum, and funeral directors might be interested too. I got on the telephone at once, and was warned that I had better be quick off the mark if I was really interested in the vehicle. Their telephone had not stopped ringing since the advertisement had appeared, and the first viewer was sure to buy. I called to see the bank manager who, whilst anything but enthusiastic, gave the go-ahead with the handicap of a strict limit on the amount I could spend. He muttered about reserves against unforeseen expenses, but I knew better and that all would be well when my cunning plan was put into operation. I was a shrewd operator by now. That same afternoon brought me to the seedy garage in a back street behind a back street.

The limousine was parked in a small enclosure, littered with vehicle parts, almost like a breaker's yard. The invitation to sit behind the wheel triggered a series of daydreams. I could see it all – brides to church, theatre parties and lucrative tours to the countryside. Tucking up Sir and Madam in cosy travelling rugs as we gently cruised along the lochside and up through the high pass on our way to visit the Laird of the Isles in his moated pile at the head of the glen. Those who would want the best of everything, probably American tourists, were my targets. We (I would obviously be included) would dine on pheasant and partridge, drink claret and single malts and not venture out at all if the weather was the least inclement. Life would be a leisurely affair and money worries a thing of the dim and distant.

My reverie was interrupted by the siren voice of the salesman, who must have known from the vacant look on my face that he had a live one here, echoing what I already knew: 'She's a real beauty all right and no mistake, isn't she, sir?' He whispered this with suitably reverential awe. 'The general's own car. Monty of El Alamein himself. It's a privilege just to sit in it. Here, try the back seat. That's where his bum used to rest between battles. It's really a shrine to the great man and should be in a museum or somewhere.' We were both struck dumb by the solemnity of it all, and then he added, 'We'll be sorry to see it go.'

As it turned out, my sentiments would become the exact opposite of his. My greatest wish would be to see it go – in a mechanical sense – but that was in the future, and for the moment I was star-struck. I was like the mother of a new baby and could not think that anyone could look at this wonderful motor and find it to be less than perfect. But I was a sharp car buyer, and so I was prepared to accept that it might require a bit of tender loving care. There was the matter of the paint job. Through the thin veneer of black paint it was possible to see the wartime camouflage markings quite clearly. I mentioned this to the salesman.

'Adds to its charm, sir. It's history made real.' It seemed a satisfactory enough explanation to me. The wide balloon desert tyres had been removed and replaced with thin spindly ones that gave the car a top-heavy look. This too I brought to the salesman's attention.

'Not suitable for city streets, sir. It's actually against the law to fit balloon tyres: makes the steering much lighter when the tyres are thinner.' As a professional driver myself I could appreciate that anything that made life easier for the driver and safer for the passengers was fine by me. I would not wish to confront the law at this stage of my business development. The big Humber was fitted with a straight six-cylinder engine and when the bonnet was lifted I have to confess to experiencing a pang of disappointment. What was not streaked in oil was rusty. The salesman must have been a trained mechanic because he instantly divined that it probably needed a new gasket. I agreed.

'Will you start it up for me?'

'Well no, it needs a battery, and then there's the matter of the gasket.' This explanation seemed reasonable enough. The salesman continued: 'We did mention in the advertisement that it needed minor repairs.' He was, of course, right again. He seemed a very reasonable chap. He then played the ace in his hand. 'Did I mention the air conditioning, sir?' No, he had not.

'Air conditioning?' I was intrigued.

'Oh yes, sir, Monty was in the desert and that and needed to keep a cool head so he could win all them battles.' I had recently spent two years in the desert myself, so I knew what he meant, but I had never heard of refrigeration in a car.

'First car in the world to have it,' lied Mr Tom Pepper, salesman extraordinaire. 'Look underneath for yourself.' An amazing array of Heath Robinson-inspired pipework of differing diameters met my uncomprehending gaze. It all looked hi-tech and superb, but I would soon master it. The salesman pointed out an undisputable fact. 'Do you no' mind seeing Monty in the newsreels, always immaculate? That was because his car was like a fridge.' Even with all this clearly expensive gadgetry aboard I would drive a hard bargain.

Scrutiny of the logbook showed that the vehicle was indeed ex-WD. There was no actual mention of Lord Montgomery, but why would the salesman lie to me? Three or four previous owners were listed, and judging by the dates of the transfers they seemed to have played a motorised version of 'pass the parcel' with it. How depressing, I thought, because if I bought it I would keep it and cherish it and I would be her last owner. This remarkable prophecy actually came to pass.

When I asked the salesman to explain the number of owners he explained that it was all part of an elaborate tax dodge. Each listed owner was in fact a director of the company and by this stratagem there were huge tax savings to be made. As he imparted this trade secret he tapped his nose with his forefinger. I was not a Freemason but understood the significance of the signal. If he was a member of the Craft then he was clearly a man who could be trusted. That was a sound piece of advice in regard to the directors, because soon I would be on the look-out for tax dodges myself. The odometer was stuck at 12,000 and the numbers were very difficult to read as they were well out of alignment. He was honest too about this situation.

'It may,' he conceded, 'have done a few more miles than shown, but not many.' The missing wind-up handle for the division could apparently be picked up anywhere for coppers. What was of more concern for me, a confirmed non-smoker like Monty, was the thick layer of evil-smelling nicotine stain on the roof cloth. His next revelation took my breath away.

'Monty was a secret smoker, did you not know? Best kept secret of the war,' affirmed the salesman. 'It just needs a wipe.' I had never realised that Monty smoked, but naturally in war all sorts of information becomes distorted. He probably wanted to keep his troops fit by the rumoured example he was said to set. It just goes to show that you can't trust anyone. The salesman hinted that Monty had been a secret drinker too. His claim was brutal. 'Monty drank more than Churchill!' We now got down to the real business in hand – the haggle over the price – and I would be no pushover, as he would find out. Unfortunately, he was called away to the telephone at that moment and I was left to cool my heels for about five minutes. I used the time to plan my strategy for putting a polish on this beauty and getting her back on the road. When the salesman returned he looked embarrassed. 'Sorry,' he said, 'but you can't have the Humber. My boss has promised it to a telephone buyer who wants it regardless of price.' I was a bit miffed.

'You can't do that. We're in the middle of negotiations and it is always first come first whatsit in business.' He nodded his head.

'You could be right.' He agreed. 'But I'll get in terrible trouble with my boss.' Then he brightened, 'Unless I say that I had already sold it to you.' This seemed an eminently suitable solution to a potentially tricky situation. However, I am no mug when it comes to buying a car and I drove him into the ground with my demands. The exhaust pipe, though not connected, I wanted. It was somewhere around and he would find it and put it in the back of the car for me. The air conditioning and the newfangled air brake system only needed to be connected. He would have to throw in the tin of polish that I demanded, and a new battery; but he haggled, and in the end I settled for a second-hand one that only needed to be recharged. By now I felt quite sorry for him when he assured me that he was liable to lose his job when his boss found out how I had bested him, what with the tin of polish and the battery and everything. The deal was done.

Bert was off-duty that day, and when I telephoned him he promised to assist me in removing the Humber. He advised me to stay with the car to make sure that none of the disconnected parts were pinched, and he would be right down. He parked his car round the corner and it was agreed that he would drive the taxi while I was towed in the new car. As it was dragged slowly from the yard I took a triumphant look through the rear-view mirror at the salesman to see how he was taking it. It was clearly not his day. The poor man must have dropped something heavy on his foot, probably a battery, because he was looking up at the sky with an arm outstretched, grimacing with pain and wiping a tear from his eye and jigging about.

If I hadn't known better I could have sworn that he was dancing.

30

AVRIL

Sunday afternoons were always a quite time for the taxi trade, and this might explain my reason for undertaking a drive to West Calder and back, a fair distance, and well beyond the city limits, enabling negotiations to take place. The taxi trade likes to be paid for every mile travelled, but only in a city like London could this be achieved. In Edinburgh most journeys were paid for only one way, and one could risk blindness by peering in all directions for a fare during a return journey. That I was prepared to transport Avril for only the fare on the clock, and charge only for one way, convinces me that I must have met Avril socially, and perhaps I must have quite fancied her. I knew nothing about her but had been promised high tea when we got there, so that might have been the incentive.

The house, belonging to her parents, was spotless, despite the presence of two small and very excited children, and was warm and cosy. Avril, an attractive girl in her late twenties, was obviously the mother of the youngsters and grandma and granddad were clearly acting *in loco parentis*. There was no trace of her husband. The subject of the conversation was her marriage. Her husband had been her childhood sweetheart, and she had been blissfully happy until he broke the eleventh commandment.

In the early years of their marriage her husband had 'worked on the tools' as the local saying goes, but being a chap with ambition he had eventually been promoted to an office-based job, wore a suit to work and had the use of a vehicle. Avril had worked part-time, and as a family unit they were on the way up. His affair was with a young girl who worked in his office, and he was so smitten with her that when caught had confessed to being in love with the young trollop. Avril had found a photo of the tart in his briefcase, signed 'with all her love'. A more experienced philanderer would have explained it away and blamed those wooden spoon merchants on the factory floor, but he was clearly a beginner and held his hands up to the charge. He had been unfaithful, and she had been with no one else ever, as she was the faithful type, and so the marriage was over. I should perhaps explain that the words 'trollop' and 'tart' were Avril's descriptions, and not those of her soon-to-be ex-husband.

The marriage was finished and early divorce was the only option, according to Avril. Her kindly parents could only, with many reservations, agree to such an action but could not contribute financially. I was included in the conversation and felt that mum and dad might be under the mistaken impression that I was being considered for the post of Mr Right. Avril made no comment as to my status. The expense of a divorce was gone into and the parents, who were clearly prepared to do all they could for their daughter, indicated that they, with the burden of two extra mouths to feed, could not help. I felt sorry for Avril, who struck me as being a thoroughly decent girl who had made a bad choice, and her life was on hold until the divorce could be sorted out. On the journey back to town she bored me rigid with her condemnation of her soon-to-be-former husband's misconduct. She was convinced that she was the only person in the world that this had happened to. She ranted on and on.

'Imagine, taking advantage of my trust. He's a swine. Lots of men have chatted me up since we got married, but I would never ever consider being unfaithful. When you get married it should be for keeps. I was a virgin when I met him and was still a virgin when we walked down the aisle. I've never been with anyone else in my life. He's a rat, that's what he is, a rat.' The tirade continued non-stop and I have to confess that I stopped listening long before we reached town. Avril was extremely attractive and I really fancied her and toyed with the idea of suggesting that the best way to get her own back on her husband would be to sleep with another man, preferably me. Something stopped me from voicing my thoughts because she was not only very strait-laced, she was hard-up and a potential divorcee with two kids in tow, not quite my idea of girlfriend potential. The other reason that stopped me from putting my idea into words was her fixation on her rat husband and the difficulty of trying to hold an intimate conversation with me in the front and her on the back seat of the taxi. Raised voices were required to overcome the clattering of the old Ferguson diesel engine, hardly conducive to whispering sweet nothings. Had we been closer I could have tried Traffic Warden Hugh's blowing-in-the-ear technique but the gods were against me. I made my contribution to her divorce fund by taking only the cost of the diesel for the trip. On the other hand, I had enjoyed a free meal so it was a fair quid pro quo.

If Avril wanted a divorce that badly she would have to get a job, perhaps two jobs, and save hard. The cost had been quoted at over £80 and that was a lot of money for anyone to find, so it would be no easy task. Whether she would save her money and secure her decree nisi I didn't know. She was certainly prepared to turn her hand to anything and work as many hours as it took to make her money and break free.

I was to be surprised.

Avril could not have been further from my mind, and it had been almost three months since my run to West Calder when I met the vet. He might not actually have been a vet, but he told me he was one and I believed him. It is disarming when a possible client admits at once that he has no money. He did not need to tell me he was drunk, but he held it well. He was in two minds as to where he wanted to be taken. He had missed the last train to wherever and faced a few hours' wait before a milk train left for his distant destination, so I felt that it could finish up as a nice little earner as an out of town trip. Finally he made his decision.

'I know,' he said. 'Take me to Dora's.' This was as near as I would ever get to an instruction to 'follow that cab' of legend. Dora was, of course, the famous brothel-keeper who had run her business from Danube Street since time immemorial. I had never been there, so I looked forward to the experience. On the way he reflected how he used to visit the premises during his student days, and he gave me an angle to consider that had not previously crossed my mind. As a student he had found study hard, and although he had a need for a woman from time to time, his brain had to focus on his studies to the exclusion of all else. Romance would have diverted his thoughts and energies, so visits to Danube Street had provided the light relief he required. A different girl was obtained on each visit, so no romantic entanglement was possible. It was a point that I could bring up for discussion in the taxi drivers' canteen in the Caledonian Station when the inevitable rows broke out over the legalisation of such places.

Once we were on our way he again mentioned that he had no money. Not that he was broke or anything like that, but Dora, knowing him as a client of long standing, would cash his cheque against the cost of female companionship and give him a float of a few pounds into the bargain.

This would be enough to pay me and he could have an early breakfast at the station. His financial embarrassment was of a temporary nature and I was not to worry. He stressed that I should pick him up no later than 5.30 in the morning to enable him to catch the milk train to his home in time for morning surgery.

I should stress that although I had been driving for some time I still had a lot to learn.and although I did not wear an 'L' plate on my back, my inexperience must have been obvious. He was a braver man than I was as he hammered on the door of the celebrated brothel in the early hours. He must have awakened the whole house, as well as the residents of several neighbouring houses, before the door was eventually opened. From the cab I could see and hear nothing, but it was obvious that he was being made welcome, and he disappeared inside. I went back to work.

When it was my turn to bang at the door a little after five in the morning I made no impression whatsoever. The houses in Danube Street were large and attractive, but undervalued as a result of Dora's activities. They were so solidly built that my frenzied hammering at the front door went unheard. In time I gave up, but I was determined to return. In daylight I felt a bit self-conscious in making my visit, but needs must. Dora answered the door herself and to me she looked like everybody's favourite granny. A grey-headed and sweet dear old lady of indeterminate age but probably, I supposed, a little over 65. I enquired about the vet.

'Oh no, dear,' she whispered. 'He did not spend the night. After the young lady obliged him he left.' Dora had a very genteel way of referring to the activities of the house. She went on to explain that her young lady lodgers were very difficult to control and, 'no again', he had not left any money to pay for his taxi fare. There was a third 'no' when I asked if she could identify him for me and a fourth when asked if she could tell me where he was from. There was, however, light at the end of the tunnel. Could she hire my taxi for a trip up to town?

She summoned her latest 'mystery' to join her on the shopping trip. A mystery was usually a young girl found loitering around a railway or bus station with nowhere to go and no money to support herself. Some were absconders from approved schools and some had simply run away from home. Almost all had had some sexual experience, but those who had no experience soon got some in exchange for a few kind words, a meal and a bed, from those who made it their business to look out for lonely young girls.

Others had heard of Dora's establishment and were willing recruits to the profession that was her business. As she was happy to explain, perhaps in justification for her actions, she was acting in the girls' best interests.

'I rig them out in essential clothing and materials – make-up, combs, toothbrushes and all manner of things – but I never buy them coats or outdoor shoes. They run off if they have coats, dear, and then they don't repay me. They are not very grateful, some of them.' To hear Dora talk, you would think she ran some government-backed charitable home for waifs and strays. This mystery was a sulky-faced girl of no more than sixteen, perhaps less, but she seemed happy enough to go along with Dora's plans for her future. Before we left a door was knocked and Dora gave instruction to an unseen assistant. 'I'm going out for a bit so will you look after things and take care of any business while I'm gone?' A voice replied in the affirmative and we set off. Dora was in a chatty mood, probably trying to impress the new girl. It was all too like the Oliver Twist story for me to be comfortable. Dora was Fagin, the girl left in charge was the Artful Dodger and the mystery was Oliver.

'This new girl I've got,' announced Dora. 'What a worker! The other girls don't stand a chance. She pounces on every client and they come back for more. Business hasn't been this good for years.' I think Dora was trying to impress on her mystery the valuable job opportunity that was available. In the last two years a new police chief had conducted a crackdown on behalf of Dora's neighbours. The value of their homes had been halved by her presence. She had served two terms in jail but it had not altered her ways a jot. Her husband had avoided any involvement by protesting that he was a working man who knew nothing of what their paying guests got up to when he was out at work or asleep. We discussed her predicament and I advised her that I had read somewhere that a brothel is only classified as such if more than one woman operates from the premises. The answer was to put a Yale lock on each door and give each tenant a rent book. The front door would have to be left unlocked like a common-stair entrance and she would be in the clear. She seemed to think that this piece of advice could be of value. Dora was completely incorrigible, and therefore almost beyond the control of the law.

When she had completed her shopping trip her last call was to see her solicitor to discuss the strategy that I had suggested. She gave me a handsome tip, so I suppose that although I did not live on immoral earnings, I benefited in a small way from them on that occasion. The tip was handsome enough for me to agree to deliver her shopping purchases to Danube Street. I rang the bell and Dora's star apprentice, the hard worker who was outdoing the rest of the girls, answered the door. To my astonishment it was Avril from West Calder, saving hard for her divorce. When I had met her parents she had stressed to them, and I suppose to me, that there had never ever been another man in her life. Her husband's conduct had driven this undoubtedly loyal wife to this. Who could blame her, since after all her husband had been unfaithful with one girl in his office? She was repaying him with interest by sleeping with the Army, the Navy and the Air Force, plus sundry passers-by.

Some time later I found out that Avril, having earned the price of a divorce and probably a little more for a rainy day, had left Dora's employment and soon after remarried and settled down once again as a devoted wife and mother.

Dora's death brought her business to an end. Prior to that the quality trade had used the front door, and the town's apprentices had completed their sex education in the gardens by the back door. Handing over a fiver at the tradesman's entrance they were introduced to Mrs Hand and her five lovely daughters by any mysteries who might be resident. It would be their only chance for a breath of fresh air due to Dora's 'no coats or outdoor shoes' policy. It was all quaintly Victorian.

Dora was indeed sitting on a fortune, because her house would nowadays be worth well in excess of a million pounds.

31

MURDER IN MIND

The McPhee had been at it again when he purchased a Jaguar Mark VII from a couple of shady customers who ran a second-hand furniture shop in Braid Place. The bawbees must have been running low because by now it had been revealed that I drove a taxi and He-Haw was trying to raise funds and was actually considering the sale of some of his stock. In his squeaky voice he made the request.

'If you're passing Braid Place, could you call in and pick up the log book for the Jaguar?' I offered to make a special run or to take him personally but he declined. 'Just when you find yourself passing will do fine.' The sporran must have been getting very thin. And so it came to pass that the following afternoon on a lovely sunny day I was in shirtsleeve order, wearing out my old RAF shirts, the ones with the fore-and-aft studs, that I experienced something new and completely foreign to my experience.

It was just before two o'clock when I arrived at Braid Place, and as I had been told that Alexander Stirling, the proprietor, lived on the premises, he would either be in the house part of the premises or reopening the shop for the afternoon in a matter of minutes. If the shop was closed, I could nip into the pub next door for a lager and lime or a shandy to kill time until it did open. As I knocked at the door I glanced at the quality of the stock and it was clear that if push came to shove there would be no chance of getting He-Haw's money back through the forced sale of that tat.

I was about to give up when I spotted a head pop out from the living quarters, have a quick look at me and bob back again. So he was in! I knocked again loudly and a different head appeared and quickly vanished also. Then a large Alsatian ran to the door and barked at me through the glass panels. Finally, the two heads with bodies attached came to the door and it was opened an inch.

'What do you want?' This was a far from friendly greeting and hardly a way to win friends and influence people to buy. I pushed my way into the shop and explained my mission. The two of them retreated out of sight into the back shop and I was left alone with the Alsatian, a mean-looking animal that was eyeing me balefully and growling menacingly. The return of Stirling, who was a former RAF policeman, and his buddy, a character named Harkness, gave me quite a turn. In a concerted rush they attacked me, and the dog, anxious not to be left out, joined in the fun. Luckily for me, the clutter in the shop meant that they had to attack side-by-side and were unable to open up two separate fronts. The first surprise punches had split my lip and bloodied my nose. I am not a fool, and realised that I should be elsewhere since the odds were against me.

It was just my luck that the door was fitted with a self-closer and had shut behind me; it would take two hands to open it – one to turn the Yale and the other to operate the door handle. It was clear that if I turned my back I would be grabbed, so I had to face the pair. The dog meantime was by far the best fighter of the four of us and had a grip on my left leg. It was very painful. I quickly concluded that I was on the proverbial hiding to nothing and took the appropriate action. At times I can be quite perceptive. My normal sunny disposition was put on the back burner and I became quite cross, ratty in fact. Dragging the dog like a ball and chain, I launched an attack and drove the pair back. Stirling then left the battle to Harkness and disappeared into the living quarters, so I was heartened since it was one down and two to go, if you counted the hound. The noise of battle and being in full view of the street had attracted spectators, and quite a few were spilling out of the pub to enjoy the action. I cannot say that I was enjoying myself, spitting blood and with a big dog eating my calf, but I was giving better than I was getting from Harkness when Stirling reappeared, armed with a double-barrelled shotgun, which he stuck into the pit of my stomach.

This altered the odds quite a bit and frightened me nearly to death. He and I had both been in the RAF but I had been on active service and I had learned a thing or two, although I had not actually put much of it into practice. An unarmed combat instructor had told me that the sideswipe of an arm was faster than the reactions of a gunman trying to pull a trigger finger. As a result, a trained soldier will always stand well back from his target, as close combat is a game for experts. I was no expert, but here was a splendid opportunity to put theory into practice, and if it failed I hoped someone would sue the Air Ministry on my behalf.

Twice before, I had disarmed rifle-wielding idiots when I was 99.9% certain that the rifles were unloaded. This time my instincts told me that it was 99 per cent certain that this shotgun was loaded in both barrels and I could see real madness and malice in Stirling's eyes. Harkness, who had been flailing away at me somewhat ineffectually and getting the odd poke for his pains, decided to leave it to Stirling while he caught his breath. The dog was so confused that it decided to bite him, which it did, much to my satisfaction. The two of them, locked together, retired to the back of the room where Harkness addressed the dog as 'good boy' in an attempt to disengage. In a sudden and beautifully synchronised move I drew my stomach in and swept the gun barrels to one side, grabbed the stock with both hands and wrenched it out of Stirling's grasp.

To prove to the world my inexperience, I made a stupid error. Instead of firing it into the air, or better still at Stirling, I threw it into the farthest corner of the room. This was idiotic because Harkness had got rid of the dog and was once again on the attack, armed with a very large knife. I dived for the door, gripped both handles and prepared to escape. It was to no avail as I was grabbed from behind and forced to turn, like Dick Whittington, to face my enemies. The melee continued, and the spectators, some holding beer glasses, enjoyed the fun. Luck, the confined space and lack of fighting room, and the fact that all three of us were basically cowards, saved the day. I was now on the verge of losing my temper as I charged forward, punching like mad and driving them back, but it was time for flight, not fight. I was getting out of the place this time even if it meant charging through the plate glass window. I quickly turned and retreated, grabbing the handle and the Yale lock simultaneously and was halfway out when a hand grabbed my detachable collar, which now became completely detached and was left behind as I fell through the door. I saw the flash of the knife and felt a sharp pain in my back and thought I heard the thud as it struck; it felt exactly like a punch as I was propelled into the street.

The crowd of spectators, now that the entertainment was over, sloped back into the pub. Stirling and Harkness must have retreated to the living quarters and I staggered the seventy yards to Braid Place police station, leaving a pretty red trail behind me. The sergeant at the desk was an old hand, but the sight of my bloodstained appearance clearly shocked him. He raised a single eyebrow in consternation before snatching the occurrence book out of blood-spotting harm's way.

My stab wound was a great disappointment, since Harkness had chickened out and must have turned the blade at the last minute. There was an indentation where the hilt had cut my back but it was not even a stitch job. By the time assistance had been summoned by radio, and Stirling and Harkness interviewed, everything was more or less back to normal. I had a few bruises and my leg was rapidly turning an interesting shade of green, but the dog's fangs had not broken the skin so a tetanus jab was not thought necessary.

Scottish law is based on Roman law, and we Scots think it is the best system in the world by far. In actual fact the law is an ass. Two witnesses are required before a complaint can be laid. It will not surprise you to know that not a single person from the public house had seen anything at all. On the contrary, it was a particularly quiet afternoon, one of the quietest on record. It was all therefore my fault and I had better watch my step. Stirling had a valid shotgun licence, so there. He was a pillar of the community, a shopkeeper and a former RAF policeman; did I know what I was saying? I had gone to his shop and attacked him and his friend, and even his dog. I was lucky that they did not want to press charges. I knew that I had certain rights and I exercised them by insisting that my comments be recorded in the occurrence book. If anyone is interested enough to look up the long-ago filed away ledger it is all there for the world to see. I told them that in my opinion Stirling was a loony and that he would undoubtedly kill someone some day. I knew, because I had seen it in his eyes. Naturally enough this statement was thought to be the ramblings of one who had come off worst in a fight that he had started.

Hector Hamish McPhee of that Ilk was completely unimpressed by my efforts on his behalf. 'So you mean to say that after all that you did not collect the log book?' he squeaked. I will not here record my reply but he came very close to being the third person to be punched by me that day. The root cause of the fuss was then revealed.

Tired of waiting for me to act, He-Haw had been offered the services, for a white five-pound note, of a head case called Henry Stuart. Stuart's claim to fame was that he was something of a safe-blower, but in fact the only time he tried it he and his accomplice between them rock-walked a huge half-ton safe across a room and sited it against a wall. They then covered it with the office carpets and carefully drilled the necessary access holes before filling them with nitro-glycerine and then retiring to what they thought was a safe distance.

The resulting explosion blew out all the windows of the building, raised the roof by several inches and at the same time rendered the pair unconscious. They came round in time to shout 'Kamarad' and raise their hands to the fire brigade, who handed them over to the police. No one could move the safe, which had remained locked despite the explosion. After the incident, a dozen large plods tried without success to move it across the room. Such is the power of fear coupled with excitement and adrenaline. Henry was a big lad but not over-endowed with grey matter, so that when he called on Stirling a few hours before I did, the negative reply which would negate the terms of his contract riled him, so he punched Stirling in the mouth. The blow broke a tooth and was accompanied with a threat to return later when the logbook had better be produced, or else. Before he made good his promise to return I had blundered into the situation.

Not long after the Braid Place incident He-Haw disappeared from the scene as rapidly as he had entered it. One day he was there, all tam o' shanter, kilt and hairy legs, and the next he was gone. He was sadly missed once the coffee mill stopped grinding in our favour. Only Mr De Marco, the genial café proprietor, was happy when we started buying our own beverages again and steady trade returned.

I have mentioned more than once that I was better dressed than the average cabbie and it did come in handy at times. One of those times was fast approaching.

I was treating myself to a chicken Maryland and exchanging banter with some of the layabouts who were lying about as usual when a small woman dressed in extremely hairy tweeds entered the café with a bundle of walking sticks under her arm. Her voice was high-pitched and reedy. It was a voice that rang a bell, as we thought that we had all heard it before. She addressed the room at large:

'I am led to believe,' she began, in as stentorian a voice as she could muster, 'that you lot sold these sticks to my son Hector, and I want his money back.' Just as snow melts away in warm sunshine so the café emptied. Not in a rush, people simply seemed to slide out of sight. The high-pitched voice continued. 'My son has not been at all well for some time, not at all well, and I must find someone called Douglas, because my Hector bought a lot of cars on his behalf and has never been paid for them.'

I had been in one fight over the idiot Hector Hamish McPhee of that Ilk and there was no way I could win against this tiny spitfire. She would not be prepared to listen if I tried to explain the facts. That my taxi was parked yards away with my name emblazoned on the door did not help my situation.

The chicken Maryland was not up to standard that night and I made a mental note to mention it to De Marco sometime, but for some odd reason I was no longer hungry. It was imperative that I start work without delay.

In January 1958, ten weeks and two days after the incident in Braid Place, Alexander Stirling shot to death his girlfriend and her one-legged invalid father in their company-owned cottage near Salvesen's Yards, where the father worked. During the frenzied shooting spree he had to reload his ten-shot rifle. He fired fifteen or sixteen bullets in all. He was apprehended in England, near Kendal on the A6, while driving a red Ford car, and the press referred to it as either the 'red car case' or the 'A6 case' (not to be confused with the Hanratty case later). In September of that year he was sentenced to death, but the bleeding-heart liberals swung into action and his sentence was commuted to life imprisonment.

Naturally enough, since he had killed only two people, in cold blood, he was let out of prison after serving a relatively short sentence. In June of 1970 he murdered again and was jailed again later that year. I should think that the penal authorities were very annoyed about his conduct and he no doubt received a good telling-off. The betting is a hundred to one that no one lost

211

his or her job over the scandal of his early release from prison. Someone lost his or her life due to that blunder, but of course, as usual, no one was to blame. He should be incarcerated for life, but you never know, he could be living next door to you at this moment under an assumed name. My advice is not to argue with that tall, elderly neighbour, since, having killed three people already, it is probably a bit of a hobby with him now and he might just be minded to add you to his list.

32

HM B&B

The first planned booking for Monty's Motor, now looking every inch a Humber limousine, had been planned in advance, but the car had other ideas, and as a result I was forced to use the taxi. I wouldn't even lose out on a night's sleep because the old couple who had hired me assured me that they were early bedders. A run to the west coast could be interesting and profitable and I would be back in time to do normal taxi work from about ten o'clock.

I was becoming a little disenchanted with taxi work but now and then, when funds were flowing, it could be enjoyable. It is a strange life, driving a taxi. In London people see it as a good career move to qualify to drive a black cab because in the metropolis business is non-stop, making it a well-paid job – one could even call it a profession. It can take three years' minimum to acquire the Knowledge and thousands of aspiring taxi drivers fail to complete the training programme. In most other cities the time taken to memorise every street, road and lane takes a much shorter period of study, and almost without exception every driver that I have known fell into taxi driving by a series of unplanned events. Once in the rut it was difficult to break free.

We arrived at the church where the wedding was to take place with plenty of time to spare. The venue was much closer to Hamilton than Glasgow, and in my suit and bow tie I mingled with the guests quite confidently. No doubt each side of the family thought I belonged to the other; I have often thought that if ever I found myself penniless I would eat well by attending weddings and funerals as an uninvited guest. However impoverished, if you are clean and tidy and your shoes are well shined, you will be made welcome by someone.

After the ceremony the reception was the usual west-coast affair, with dancing and drinking playing a prominent part in the festivities at the local Co-operative Hall. I could not get really interested and had to avoid drinking with a night's work ahead. My elderly couple were enjoying themselves and kept assuring me every half-hour that they would be ready to leave in half an hour. As time passed I found myself going downhill fast from a bug that had been in my system for a day or two. What had started as sniffles had quite suddenly developed into a recurrence of the malaria I had suffered in Egypt. Either that, or I was suffering from a virulent strain of flu, and I was anxious to be homeward-bound. Sweat was pouring from me but I was cold and shivery. My total alcohol consumption had been a miserly two half-pints of lager and lime, and they must have exited through my pores as sweat. On their next visit to reassure me that they would not be long the old man noticed my glistening brow and became concerned.

'You've got the flu, there's a lot of it about,' he announced. 'But not to worry. I'll cure you in a jiffy.' He disappeared and returned with some Beechams powders and a large glass containing brown liquid. 'Try three of these,' he instructed. 'When I was a medic in the navy we never had cases of flu. This sovereign remedy never fails.' I meekly agreed, as I was feeling rotten. The three packets of Beechams powders were poured together and then tipped into my mouth. The brown liquid was to wash them down. When I feel well Beechams powders taste awful, but when I am under the weather they aren't so bad. I swirled the brown liquid round my mouth and swallowed the triple dose.

'Get the rest down you.' The order came from the former nursing assistant. It was nearly a full half-pint of liquid and tasted foul.

'What was that?' I spluttered, with my eyes smarting.

214

'Grog, lad, Woods rum and water. Cure anything, that will.'

I had to admit that the results were almost instantaneous. My toes warmed up first and the heat travelled upwards. I did not feel at all well but I did sense an improvement. My host was not done with me yet.

'Drink this slowly and you'll be as right as rain.' I demurred. There was no possibility that I could drink another half-pint of grog and keep it down, but he insisted that his experience would triumph. 'It's not grog this time. It's green ginger to warm you up.' He was actually telling a lie. It was green ginger, which is mildly alcoholic, mixed with equal quantities of navy rum as powerful as dynamite. It was good when sipped, and went down a treat. I felt better with every minute that passed. The reason for my fare's kindness was slipped into the conversation. 'We've been offered a bed for the night, and we're having such a good time that we've decided to stay over.' I was feeling much better – even carefree – and it was my cue to depart.

The hard night's work that I had thought lay ahead would be reduced due to the old couple's time-wasting and it would hardly be worthwhile to turn out by the time I got home. As I set off for home the grotty feeling slowly began to return, but the medicine was still fighting it on my behalf. Snow is strange stuff, and Eskimos are said to have dozens of words to describe the different kinds. This stuff that had started to fall quite gently had a hypnotic effect as it appeared through the light from the head-lamps of the taxi and rushed at the windscreen. The headlights on an FX3 were designed to work in an urban environment, where streetlights carry most of the load. On a dark country road they seemed like candles. The result was I could hardly see ahead at all and decided to pull off the road at the first opportunity and wait until the snow had stopped falling. This particular fall of snow was heavy and the road was an inch deep in no time at all. After crawling along slowly for a few minutes I came across an entry into a field, pulled off the road and parked up. I switched off the lights but kept the engine running in the hope that a little warmth would percolate through to my cabin. The taxi had a heater of sorts, but any improvement in temperature was directed to the rear compartment for the benefit of passengers. I cocooned myself in the duffel coat and pulled the hood tightly round my head as my shivering returned with a vengeance. I closed my eyes in my misery.

There are many types of wake-up calls available. They range from the strident clanging of the bell on an alarm clock to the gentle strains of soothing music on a radio alarm. A friendly telephone company will ring you up at an agreed hour, and in Lancashire and Yorkshire there are obliging 'knocker-uppers' who will bang on your windows to wake you. They ensure that you will not be late at the pit or the mill and can be relied upon to keep knocking until you open the curtains and give them a wave. What I cannot recommend is the one that woke me on that fateful night: blue flashes from strobe lighting on the roof of a police car and the door yanked open to admit sub-zero temperatures. The ignition light was on but the engine had died and I was literally freezing, perhaps to a premature death. Plods are not polite people, particularly when you involve them in paperwork during a back shift. They much prefer to huddle round the heater in their police cars. They dragged me out of the taxi, threw me into the rear seat of their car and took me to a police station in the middle of nowhere. Their sergeant was a much nicer type.

'Been drinking, have we, sir?' was his rather civil welcome. 'Come away ben and have a warm at the fire.' I was ushered into a room where a fire was roaring in the grate and where the coal was obviously purchased by the local authorities. There must have been half a hundredweight of anthracite blazing away and the heat was terrific. I am not the brightest person in the world but I did realise that in the circumstances coldness was my friend. Why I thought this is unclear, but I must have read it somewhere.

'I have certainly not been drinking,' I protested vehemently. 'I have had some medicine prescribed by a medical man. You can take that as a fact.' To call the old navy scab-lifter a medical man

216

was stretching a point, but under the circumstances it was every man for himself. My mind was quite clear.

'The three of us think that you've had a drink.' The sergeant was extremely opinionated and quite clearly did not accept my word. 'We'll need to send for a doctor. Have you a particular choice?' This was becoming serious. If I had been asked to walk a white line or work out change from a pound I would have had no problem at all; but a doctor, blood samples and all that jazz were a bit frightening. I remembered the kind offer of my bagpipe-playing Asian doctor friend.

'Yes I do,' I insisted, and I gave the address, cursing myself for not carrying his telephone number with me. I felt that, if he were not under the influence of drink himself, he would turn out. Even though I was hardly a good friend, I had at least done him a favour. Ten minutes later the sergeant reappeared.

'No reply from that number, I'm afraid.' I knew he was lying, and he knew that I knew that he was lying.

'There has to be a reply, because he's the police surgeon in Edinburgh. Even if he's not available he will have a locum on duty and an answering machine.' I had seen the newfangled gadget when I'd brought him back from Hawick. 'If he really is not available then try another doctor.' I gave the address of the family GP who had served my family for at least twenty years. The sergeant left the room and his two subordinates did likewise, no doubt in search of a cup of tea. I was sitting as far from the fire as possible when a little old lady, her hair in curlers, entered the room carrying a large leather bag. I thought it only polite to give her a suitable greeting.

'Have they caught you as well, missus?'

She was not amused and her frosty reply put me in my place 'I'm the local police doctor and I've been called to examine you,' she announced in a prim, thin-lipped way. I was pretty sure that I knew my rights.

'I'm really sorry you've been inconvenienced. I hope you get a turnout fee because I shall certainly not require your services.'

She left the room with a vinegary expression on her humourless face and with not even a nod in response to my politeness. The sergeant reappeared and effortlessly slipped into the 'I'm your friend' character.

'Look here,' he wheedled. 'You might as well let her examine you now that she's here. If you're fine then you can drive off home right away.' He had walked into my trap, I thought.

'I feel fine, so I'd like to go now if you don't mind. I would be happy to be seen by a doctor of my choice, but since you say neither is available I'll do without. I'll just go home if you'll arrange transport back to my taxi.' He was determined to be a spoilsport.

'It doesn't work like that, sir.' At least he was calling me 'sir' now. He must have been impressed by my claimed familiarity with two medical men. He probably thought that a third had prescribed my medicine. 'If you don't let the lady doctor examine you we'll lock you up for the night.' I declined his kind offer and was lodged for the night in a small room with bars on the window and a heavy steel door. It had a bed of sorts, and was en suite as far as a toilet was concerned, but the flushing chain dangled outside the cell door.

The constable who ushered me to my boudoir returned my wishes when I bade him goodnight. He took with him my belt in case I might be tempted to hang myself.

I had noisy neighbours, a consignment of gypsies, but managed to snatch a bit of sleep. In the morning I asked the police escort from the day shift to confirm that I had not asked for the chain to be used during the night but he did not appear to have any interest. When I think about it now I wonder what I was trying to prove. A night in a cell has an unsettling effect on the best of us. The breakfast was a disappointment and could have been better. A single bread roll spread with margarine and raspberry jam. The tea was watery, milky and pre-sweetened. I like my breakfast tea strong and without sugar. The meal was not a success.

A bow tie at night looks quite good but at seven in the morning it is a bit out of place. A quick swill in cold water and no shave and I was ready to go. My Irish gypsy neighbours were handcuffed to each other in line and the police escort, explaining that by rights he should handcuff me too, waived the option.

'It's not necessary seeing as how you're a gentleman,' was his explanation. The bow tie obviously had him fooled. We drove to court and eventually I was brought up from underground into the dock. It was a new experience for me. I failed to describe myself as of no fixed abode and ran the risk of the item appearing in the Edinburgh newspapers. As it turned out it was not worth the editor's ink. Had I used that ruse I would not have been bailed, so the law is not such an ass as the public believes. An elderly gentleman in a long wig asked me how I pleaded. In a firm voice, a voice that did not reflect how I felt, I pleaded not guilty. I was remanded on my own surety, whatever that meant, until six months hence, when the whole thing would be examined in detail. The date at the end of the remand coincided with my birthday, and in my elation I laughed aloud and joked with my escort that it was an early birthday present as we made our way back down the stairs. A voice from on high instructed us to 'BE QUIET DOWN THERE'.

A worried-looking policeman, who had been in the court when my laughter was heard, hurried down to join us and told my escort that the judge had made a note of the jocularity in his ledger. I was sure to catch it when I appeared in court proper. I left the building without a clue as to where I was. I went back in to ask where I had come from and where my vehicle might be located, but it was pay-back time for the plod. No one knew anything at all about it. It took several telephone calls and a good two hours to locate the police station where my cab was being held. I had six months to sort something out and was very subdued and did not laugh much on the drive back to Edinburgh.

33

DONALD'S DOPPELGÄNGER

The General Assembly of the Church of Scotland was in full swing, if that is the right word. Lots of clerical collars used taxis but none seemed to understand the concept of tipping. What a cheerless bunch they were, and the town seemed full of serious-faced men who thought that smiling was sinful. When they spoke it was in the voice that they used from the pulpit: slow, sonorous and boring to the ear. If they were ever cheerful it was late at night when sober-suited gentlemen, smelling of drink, were decanted into small back-street hotels. They were a poor advertisement for churches in general and seemed to live a life devoid of joy. For people who sang the praises of a life hereafter, and the joys that would be available in heaven, they appeared to be clinging on to earthly life with every fibre of their being. If I had been consulted – which naturally enough I wasn't – the retiring age for all churchmen of every denomination would be brought down and smiling lessons *de rigeur*. No smoking or drinking, no swearing either, and – God forbid – not even a thought of the other were the orders of the day every day for these cheerless souls. The air of doom and gloom that hung over them was catching and even the taxi-trade operators were strangely subdued as long as they were in town. Perhaps there is an element of truth in the old chestnut about the po-faced minister of the Church of Scotland being turned away from the pearly gates by St Peter since the chore of making porridge for one would be far too much trouble.

Fortunately there was a lot of other business to be had and this week was a busy one. So busy were the streets that I found myself in a traffic jam in Hanover Street while trying to get to a Princes Street rank. At the time my cab was fortunately free of passengers. I was looking around in the hope of finding a fare when I saw, for the first time in over three months, the unmistakable head of Highland Donald bobbing its way up Hanover Street towards George Street. He still owed me two pounds from the night that Moira had dashed off with his cash. When I caught up with him I would add ten bob for interest and demand two pounds and ten shillings. I was completely stuck in traffic, so when a tiny space at the nearside pavement opened up I slipped in and abandoned the cab. I sprinted up the street in pursuit. Two pounds plus would be much happier in my pocket than his. Perhaps he had forgotten that hiss word was supposed to be hiss bond; well I'd remind him. I hated the thought of being taken for a sucker by a sucker. I'd have his guts for garters. Driving a taxi does nothing for a man's fitness and even the 50-yard dash had me out of breath. But there would be no escape for the lanky Donald. Moira was definitely right; he was a creep. As I got closer, pushing my way through the pedestrians crowding the pavement, I became aware that I was seeing double. There were two identical heads bobbing up and down in unison. Both necks were encased in identical university scarves trailing nearly to the ground behind them. Every step brought me closer to my money. I caught up with them and for a second or two I couldn't tell which of them was the Donald I was after. One head of hair was grey so I went for the younger man. Grabbing his arm I swung him round and blurted out.'Right you! What about my money? You've been dodging me!' With that, my opening sally, I abruptly stopped talking. Donald and his companion were clones. Identical in height, weight and cloth-ing. The elder was greyer, his face more lined, but two peas from the same pod, without a doubt.

'Erg!' came a strangled cry from Donald as his face turned first chalk-white, then the old familiar green tinge from the gills, before flushing into a bright crimson of embarrassment. The older lookalike looked at me with interest. His solemn face was kindly but concerned. In stopping so suddenly and turning towards me their identical scarves fell open to reveal matching dog collars. Both carried similar large black leather-bound Bibles. Donald must have passed his exams and been ordained into some joyless Highland church. It was no time to argue about money or bring up his recent past, certainly not in front of his father.

'Sorry,' I mumbled. 'My mistake, I thought you were someone else.' As I retraced my steps to the abandoned taxi a few things became clear. Highland Donald will be approaching retirement age now but is no doubt still preaching hell and damnation to his flock. He will be a pillar of his local community. But just remember, Donald, if you should read this, you still owe me £2.

As for me, visits to the church have never been quite the same; I keep wondering if the minister has a complete pocket in his trousers and what might he have got up to during his student days?

34

STORMY WEATHER

It was the night of the great storm. All day long the weather reports had become increasingly pessimistic and warned, with due solemnity, that the weather was worsening and we could expect the most ferocious storm conditions recorded for years, and that this nightmare was definitely on its way. Structural damage was certain and hatches were to be battened down. Everyone thought they were ready for it . . . until it struck. The barometer readings dropped like a stone and bounced on the bottom of the scale. The wind rose and rose again alarmingly, its voice becoming louder and louder. With it came rain of monsoon intensity, drenching everything and pouring down like a wall of solid water, the wind shifting it this way and that. Some said that it was the worst weather in living memory, whilst others claimed that it was the worst since record-keeping began. It was a night I will always remember.

My night shift was due to begin at 6 p.m. but it was a Sunday, usually a quiet day for business, and it was almost 7.30 before I made my way carefully to the Caledonian Station through the dark and empty streets. The wind was still rising and the gusts that entered the open side of the taxi shoved the whole vehicle (weighing nearly a ton and a half) all over the road. Control was out of the hands of the driver at such times and it was a danger-ous situation for everyone: driver, passenger or pedestrian. There were, however, no passengers or pedestrians; they had enough sense to stay at home. The corporation had withdrawn public transport, something that was almost unheard-of, and taxis might be needed in emergency situations. The newspapers used us at times like this to drive their reporters to sites of newsworthy incidents. High-sided vehicles had been blown over and at Binns at the West End a plate-glass window had been blown in, and then out, and the huge sheet of glass, weighing several hundredweights, was left leaning against the outside wall of the building. If it fell on a pedestrian it would kill for certain. I was delighted to arrive at the station safely, but the news was not good. Trees were being blown down all over the country and roads and railway lines were blocked as a result.

Very few taxis had bothered to turn out and it promised to be a disappointing night for those of us who had made the effort. Criminals were having a night off too, and policemen, snug in their little boxes, drank tea to pass the time. Trade was dead, and even the church doors, in this God-fearing city, were closed and barred. Having a shrewd idea that I was wasting my time I decided, after commiserating with the few other drivers on duty, that a slow trawl along Princes Street was my only option. If the Waverley Station was as dead as the Caledonian then it was hot cocoa and bed, and someone else could handle any emergency work that turned up. It would be the first time that I had failed to earn even a penny on a shift. As it turned out, the sales figure would become a minus.

New regulations had come into force obliging us to turn left out of the Caledonian Station, and as I rounded Rutland Square a chimney pot crashed down from five storeys above to explode like a howitzer shell right in front of the taxi. A moment sooner and it would have landed on top of me, with disastrous effect. Chimneys look small from street level but close up they are frighteningly big. Slates, lethal as guillotine blades, knifed through the air, raining down potential death to the unwary or unlucky, so this was no place for me. It was a very dark night, made blacker by the rain-filled clouds at zero feet. In Shandwick Place the street lamps swayed alarmingly and some, suspended from cross-street wires, leapt and jumped about in a mad, frightening, macabre dance. Rivers of water sluiced down the gutters, completely overwhelming the street drainage system. When the taxi entered the open space where the five roads converged at the West End of Princes Street, we seemed to enter the eye of the storm and for just a moment all was calm. A few yards more and the tornado gathered the taxi up in a violent hand and shook it fiercely. Dustbins, benches, newspaper placards and all kinds of lethal debris swirled about, and I caught the incongruous sight of a double page of dry newspaper, from who knows where, suddenly gust up into the air. Higher and higher it flew in the up-draught of the storm's centre, just like a kite, 50 or 60 feet or maybe more, only to be caught in a great wave of rain and dashed to the ground in an instant, literally shredded to oblivion before my startled eyes. Huge dollops of water were bouncing knee-high off the road and it was all I could do to keep the cab moving in a semblance of a straight line. The windscreen wipers were no match for a deluge like this and I had to peer owlishly, face close to the screen, to find my way safely through the darkness. I was fearful of damaging my beloved LYO350. Out of the corner of my eye I caught sight of a figure darting out of a doorway and holding up an arm for me to stop. I think that I was as surprised to see her as she was to see me. Before the cab had stopped properly she was inside and laughing out loud.

'My God,' she exclaimed. 'Am I glad to see you! I was beginning to think that I was the last person on earth; where is everybody?' Before I had a chance to answer she gabbled on. 'I know a couple of taxi drivers and I hoped you were one of them. I want you to take me to Joppa, or as near there as you can, for twelve and sixpence. It's all I've got.' She sat sideways on one of the tip-up seats so that we could talk and be heard above the storm. 'By the way,' she announced, 'my name is Sam, and before you ask, I'm an octoroon.' I had not set eyes on her yet but she was so chatty that it would have been churlish to ignore her. I told her my name was Doug and that I was very pleased to meet her. I did not know where Octoroon was, but guessed it was in Africa or Asia, and wisely kept my mouth shut on the subject. Her next remark floored me, but might partly explain the outcome of our meeting. 'I'm a bastard as well, but the good-natured sort.' Such candour was beyond my experience and I presumed that it was a sympathy plea to ensure that she would be delivered to her doorstep. She was perfectly safe since I wouldn't have turned a sea dog out on a night like this.

'Don't worry,' I reassured her. 'I'll take you to your door.'

'You're a pet,' she said. 'I thought you might. Anyway, my husband is a furniture delivery driver and he's stuck somewhere near North Berwick. The police will not allow high-sided vehicles to move so he's there for the night. When he phoned me he said that there's dozens of cars and lorries all over the place and he's staying where he is for as long as he has to. He won't be home until breakfast time at the earliest, but more likely after lunch. With him away I decided to nip out and have a drink or two. That's my story, what's yours?'

My story was duller. A new second-hand taxi owner trying to make a crust and keep up the payments on the cab. The town being dead, it was home to bed.

Sam was a talker and it transpired that her idea of Joppa was actually the outskirts of Musselburgh, and by the time we got there I had discovered that an octoroon was someone who was one-eighth coloured. Her father could have been a half-caste, a seaman for instance, and her mother white. Sam was a mine of irrelevant information. She had been brought up in Geordieland in a variety of foster and children's homes. A series of 'uncles' had interfered with her from the age of eight, something I could not believe would happen in council-run homes, but now we all know better, and as a consequence her life had been hard and unhappy. Her marriage was 'so-so', and since we were now such firm friends it would be mean to take her twelve and sixpence and leave her penniless until her husband returned. The subject of a small loan was raised. Memories of Lynn rushed to mind, and the link between her request for a loan and her tragic death still troubled me greatly, but I was still as tight as ever – meanness being essential to my survival as a cab owner. So I produced only my slimmer wallet. Surprise, surprise; trade being practically nonexistent, it contained thirty shillings only. I was still naïve enough to believe that loans should be repaid and I was not at all sure that my new friend Sam subscribed to that view.

'That's more than enough to see me through until my husband gets back.' Sam assured me. 'I wouldn't dream of asking but I don't know when he'll be back and twelve and sixpence is not much use is it?' I had now had a chance to have a proper look at Sam, and I liked what I saw. Apart from jet-black eyes and what looked like tanned skin, there was nothing exotic about her, but she was slim and attractive, fairly small and decidedly friendly. When we arrived at her home I was invited inside, an invitation I gratefully accepted, and hot coffee was the order of the day. She had a headscarf on and when she removed this and shook her head long tresses of black hair cascaded over her shoulders. Sam was more attractive than I had thought, and she could cook too. Well, perhaps not cook, but she produced two steaming mugs in no time at all.

In the *News of the World* Sunday newspaper in the 1950s their intrepid reporters, having got into the type of situation that I was in, would make their excuses and leave. I was not a newspaper reporter and was not in the mood to leave the warmth and attractiveness of the situation, so a discreet veil must be drawn over the subsequent proceedings.

When I did leave the storm had abated. We were both keen to have further meetings and, tired as I was, I was obliged to pay attention to Sam's instructions. They were quite specific and seemed to me complicated.

'Don't telephone first. Just call round anytime, and if the van is not parked right in front of the house, we can have some fun. Leave your taxi a few streets away, because you know what neighbours can be like. The only time not to call when the pantechnicon is away is if the bedroom curtains are drawn shut. I'm a nurse and sometimes I have to work nights and I have to catch up on my beauty sleep. You will remember, because it's very important.' Sam certainly could talk. I had always believed that nurses were hot stuff and now it had been proved. What a girl. Sam's strange sets of rules were committed to memory and I crept back out into the remains of the storm. As I drove home I was elated. I had heard drivers boast about their girlfriends and supposed conquests of happily married women who were ready and willing to have uncomplicated non-emotional relationships. I had cracked it, I had Sam. She was mine, and mine alone, just as long as hubby was away. But that was our secret.

When I surfaced the following afternoon it was as if the storm had never been. Was the whole thing a figment of my imagination? A dream? The air was still and the weather warm and vaguely sunny in a watery sort of way. The passion of the storm had gone, but my head was full of Sam. How soon could I pay another visit without appearing to be too eager? In the end I decided to play it cool. I would wait until I had a hire taking me near Musselburgh before calling. What if I trailed all that way only to find the furniture van in place or the curtains drawn against me? No, on balance it was better not to be over-anxious. I did not want to become too infatuated. If only she lived in the centre of town things could be different, but I would be patient.

By Thursday I was desperate to see her and I determined to take a run to Musselburgh that night and take a chance on disappointment. Before setting off I would get a good meal inside me. A new café had recently opened on Buccleuch Street and I had heard good reports about the food from other cabbies. When I approached it was clear that the gossips had been right. The grub must be good and reasonably priced because a dozen taxis were parked along the street by the café. As I entered I was in a kind of dreamland, thinking of nothing other than the delightful Sam and our secret. I had only just sat down when I was wrenched from my reverie by a prolonged burst of applause, cheering and whistling from the assembled cabbies. I thought that it must be someone's birthday, but it became clear that I was the object of their interest. Drivers, some of whom I had never met before, were queuing up to shake my hand while others patted me on the back. What was going on? A spokesman took over.

'Here he is, lads. Every driver in town has been looking out for him. A credit to the taxi trade, if ever there was one. I give you the one, and the only, the seven-timer!'

35

EPILOGUE

Taxi! has been written at long last, and I'm surprised to find that I have only started to tell the story . . . At this point perhaps I should tell readers that the second instalment of *Taxi!* has been written and that Charlie the Gangster, PC Bert, Pedro the Pirate, Farouk, Tommy and others will reappear in its pages.

Readers will also find out the future of Monty's Motor, the outcome of my legal problem, and can look forward to meeting a whole range of new and interesting characters. All stories have endings, but I have to confess that in some cases I don't know how they finished. About some others I can enlighten you.

Avril and her new husband disappeared from view and we can presume that they both lived happily ever after. The Regional Commander of the Scottish Republican Army failed in his attempt to reach for the stars and might well be residing in a secure home for the bewildered. Big Tam became one of the most famous 'filum' stars in the world. The irrepressible Michael and Mary, despite their temporary setback, carried on regardless. Highland Donald took himself back to the Highlands, well away from the temptations of Edinburgh. Scouse is still doing the rounds. These comments refer to the time period following their appearances in *Taxi!* By the time the book is published most will be either dead or in God's waiting room. Should they recognise themselves they are unlikely to sue me. Why? Because every story is true, and apart from that, few authors have any money.